Faith–Catch It

Knowing About It Is Not Enough

by
Scott Webb

Harrison House
Tulsa, Oklahoma

10 09 08 07   10 9 8 7 6 5 4 3 2 1

Faith–Catch It
Knowing About It Is Not Enough
ISBN 13: 978-1-57794-864-3
ISBN 10: 1-57794-864-5
Copyright © 2007 by Scott Webb
100 Derby Parkway
Birmingham, AL 35210

Published by Harrison House, Inc.
P.O. Box 35035
Tulsa, Oklahoma 74153
www.harrisonhouse.com

Table of Contents

Preface

*We having the same **spirit of faith,** according as it is written, I believed, and therefore have I spoken; we also believe, and therefore speak.*

2 Corinthians 4:13 (emphasis mine)

The Word of God concerning faith revolutionized my life. I caught that spirit of faith over thirty years ago, and I've been walking in it ever since; but as a child and even through my teen years I was never taught these truths. Although my family attended church regularly, back then we were not taught much, if anything, about faith. Consequently, I had very little understanding about the things of God or the Word of God, and it wasn't long before I got away from God altogether. As a result, I went through some rough years.

When I came back to Jesus and decided to get my life in order, the call of God on my life became obvious. I knew it had been there since I was a young child, and I began searching for answers, for direction. That's when I heard the message of faith in God for the first time; that is, the life and lifestyle of faith. I never will forget it. After being raised in religion that had no power or substance of faith, the truth of God's Word took hold of me and came alive in me.

God later spoke to my heart and said, "The subject of faith can be *taught,* but the spirit of faith must be *caught!*" Light came and I saw it! I caught the spirit of faith, and revelation of God's Word began to flow in me. I saw that the spirit of faith speaks, and speaking God's Word brought His power to bear in every situation I faced then and continues to bring victory in everything I face today.

This book will give you an understanding of the difference between knowing about faith and having the *spirit* of faith. When you know the difference, you too can catch the spirit of faith. It is the life-changing, faith-speaking, devil-defeating, spirit of power that compels you to act on God's Word and never give up, shut up, or put up with anything that is not of God!

I encourage you to open your heart to the principles from the Word of God taught in this book, studying them again and again until you catch the sprit of faith. It will transform your thinking, your actions, and reactions from the inside out—just like it has me and countless others. I promise you, your life in Jesus Christ will move into dimensions of joy and power you never imagined! Catch it!

CHAPTER 1

Faith Works by Love

I want to begin by sharing a truth that is vital to understanding God's Word concerning faith and to receiving from Him by faith. Without revelation of this essential truth, your very relationship with God will be hindered. This truth is found in Galatians 5:6, which says that *faith works by love.*

In very simple terms, the Holy Spirit is teaching us that when we understand how much God loves us, it is natural and easy to have faith in Him, to trust His Word, and to believe He is faithful to fulfill His promises to us. On the other hand, if we do not know and understand that God loves us, it is hard to believe that He will bless us, that He wants to bless us, or that He will do what He promises to do in His Word.

Some who teach faith have failed to teach this first and most important principle: God is love and He loves us. It is easy to assume that those we teach have this basic understanding of God's love and mercy, but many people have been taught that

God is vengeful and out to get them. If that is what they believe about Him, they will think that anything bad or hurtful is an act of God to punish them or to teach them something. They will have no faith in Him or His Word to bless them by delivering them, healing them, and giving them His wisdom and strength to resist every temptation and overcome every trial. That is why an understanding of the love of God is so vital to our faith.

Once we get a revelation of the very nature of God—that He is love, that He is merciful, forgiving, and always wants to bless us and provide for us—then we can begin to know Him as a loving Father who would never harm or punish us. We live in a fallen world that produces trouble, and if we yield to sin there will be consequences to bear. Knowing we have a Heavenly Father who is there to help us through the trials and temptations of life, who is always for us and never against us, is one of the foundations of our faith that sustains us. Instead of turning away from Him or blaming Him in times of trouble or temptation, we will run to Him and receive His mercy and grace.

Without this basic knowledge, the life of faith is often grossly reduced to religious formulas that lack true intimacy with the God of the Bible as the basis of believing. You may have heard messages on seven steps for health, five steps to success, and eight steps to prosperity. Sadly, most of these formulas leave out personal communication with God. What is worse, some believers get hold of these formulas without ever completely surrendering themselves to the will and Word of

God. The life of faith then becomes an exercise in greed and self-centeredness. When it doesn't work for them and they don't get what they want, it is easier to say this teaching is false doctrine than to submit themselves to God, open their hearts to Him, and find out what the Word of God and the Spirit of God are saying to *them personally.*

Knowing, submitting to, and walking in daily communion with our Heavenly Father and His Word establish us in His love. Study and prayer give us a solid understanding that faith works by love according to Galatians 5:6, and that according to 1 John 4:16, God is love. The Bible clearly speaks about a love relationship with God, and daily communion with Him builds the foundation of our faith. Without the confidence in our hearts that God loves us and wants only good for us, our faith in Him is rendered ineffective; but the knowledge that God loves us and is faithful to His Word generates powerful faith.

Where Love Begins

Many have taught that faith works by love, and that failure to walk in love toward others will cause your faith to be unproductive. That is true. In Mark 11:25, for example, Jesus mentioned that unforgiveness will stop faith from working. When we hold an offense and harbor resentment toward someone, we are not walking in love and our faith is made ineffective by unforgiveness. Therefore, it is important that we walk in love toward our brothers and sisters in Christ and toward those around us. But there is an even more fundamental truth that needs to be embraced by the believer in order to love and forgive others.

First John 4:19 says, "We love him, because he first loved us." Any unconditional love you have in your heart for God, for yourself, or for others comes from Him. God is the initiator of love because He *is* love. You simply respond to His love, enjoy His love for you, and express His love to others. God doesn't wait for you to do something right so He can love you. He is continually extending and expressing His love for you, which is the foundation of your faith and the basis upon which you believe His promises.

One thing that will help establish your heart in the love of God is praying the prayers in the Book of Ephesians over yourself. These prayers speak of being "rooted and grounded in love."

Let's look at the prayer in Ephesians, chapter 3.

For this cause I bow my knees unto the Father of our Lord Jesus Christ,
Of whom the whole family in heaven and earth is named,
That he would grant you, according to the riches of his glory, to be strengthened with might by his Spirit in the inner man;
That Christ may dwell in your hearts by faith; that ye, being rooted and grounded in love,
May be able to comprehend with all saints what is the breadth, and length, and depth, and height;

And to know the love of Christ, which passeth knowledge, that ye might be filled with all the fulness of God.

Now unto him that is able to do exceeding abundantly above all that we ask or think, according to the power that worketh in us,

Unto him be glory in the church by Christ Jesus throughout all ages, world without end. Amen.

Ephesians 3:14-21

This prayer holds true for us today because, even though Paul wrote it, the Holy Ghost inspired him to pray it and write it for our benefit. The heart of God inspired Paul to pray this way, so we ought to take a close look at it and see what the Holy Spirit is really praying through us when we pray it.

I want to call your attention to verse 17, where Paul prayed that Christ may dwell in our hearts by faith and that we will be rooted and grounded in love. Then verse 19 tells us that in order to be filled with the fullness of God, we must first know the love of Christ. Paul also said that knowing the love of Christ passes knowledge. In other words, the love of God is *beyond the ability of the natural mind to comprehend.* Our natural minds cannot grasp it because it is a spiritual truth.

Now let's read Ephesians 3:19 from *The Amplified Bible.*

...[That you may really come] to know [practically, through experience for yourselves] the love of Christ, which far surpasses mere knowledge [without experience].

It is one thing to talk about God's love in an abstract way, like in the children's song, *Jesus Loves the Little Children.* That song speaks of God's love for all the children, all over the world. But it is another thing to *experience God's love yourself.* You must know and understand firsthand, without any doubt, that God loves YOU.

In verse 17 we read that knowing God and His fullness begins with being rooted and grounded in love. Rooting and grounding speaks of a foundation. The foundation of faith is an understanding of God's love and the love of Christ for YOU. Love begins to work in your life when you get a revelation of His love for you, and only then can you return His love and walk in love toward others.

God Loves YOU

Before you can really walk in love toward others—including God—you have to understand for yourself that God loves YOU. Love is a big word with many different meanings. We know there are different Greek words translated "love" in the New Testament, and each has a different meaning. In Ephesians, chapter 3, the word used is *agape,* which means love and affection in the sense of benevolence, the unconditional love that is unique to God.[1] The God kind of love is love without strings attached. God loves you because that's just the way He is! It is not based on your character or your performance. It is based on His nature. He is love.

Why do we have such a difficult time understanding that God loves us just the way we are? As we saw in verse 19, God's love is a love that "passeth knowledge" and cannot be comprehended by our natural minds. Only after we are born again and spiritually connected to God can we begin to experience and understand deep in our hearts the miracle of His unconditional love for us.

Even after we are saved we can struggle with the idea that God loves us no matter what we think, say, or do. Yet we hear preaching and teaching about how God is love and we say amen with everyone else. We introduce unbelievers to Jesus by telling them how much God loves them, that He loved them so much He gave His only Son, Jesus, to die for their sins. We tell them that Jesus loved them so much He willingly suffered and laid down His life to pay for their sin and bring them into right standing with God. However, when it comes to walking in complete faith and trust in God and His Word in our everyday lives, we often stumble because of wrong thinking, such as, *God loves everybody but me. I'm not really good enough. I'm not living right enough, haven't prayed enough, or I'm not worthy.* These thoughts are lies, perpetrated by the devil to stop us from walking in love and faith toward God.

The devil knows that if he can convince us that we are not good enough for God to love us, then it is easy for us to believe that God doesn't love us enough to heal us, deliver us, or prosper us. We will have no faith in Him to perform His Word in our lives. If you have believed that lie, the Holy Spirit wants you to know this: God loves YOU—*no strings attached!*

You have to embrace God's unconditional love for you personally. It is easy to hide yourself in a church or group of believers who are on fire for God and full of faith for miracles. It's very easy to rejoice in God's love and goodness when you are among others who are rejoicing. But when it's just you by yourself and trouble comes, what do you think? What do you really believe? What do you say and pray? And what do you do as a result of what you think, believe, and say?

When a problem arises in your family and you aren't surrounded by a congregation of worshipping saints and the leaders of your church, do you know and believe what God's Word says? Do you know and believe God loves you and wants to help you, and that all His promises are *yes* and *amen* for you? In order to fully believe that, you've got to have a revelation, an understanding that goes past mere knowledge into experience, with the truth that God loves YOU no matter what you have said or done or how you have failed.

You can begin by simply confessing and coming into agreement with the Word of God that says God loves you. Say it over and over to yourself throughout the day and as you are going to sleep at night. Say, "God loves me. God loves ME! Thank You,

Father, for loving me so much. Thank You, Holy Spirit, for pouring out God's love in my heart." (Romans 5:5.)

Don't Believe the Lie!

Having faith in God and His Word doesn't have to be hard. First, consider the faith you have for others. When an unbeliever comes to you and says, "I've been so bad. I've done so much wrong. How could God love me or forgive me?" what do you always tell them?

"No way!" you answer boldly and confidently. "God's love is so much bigger than anything you've said or done. There's nothing that you could possibly do that is bigger than the love of God or greater than the blood Jesus shed for you. And His sacrifice reveals the depth and breadth of His love for you." You have probably led people to Jesus and comforted doubting, tormented believers with these words—and then forgot that they also apply to you!

When we think about God's love, sometimes we picture innocent little children. I have four grandchildren, and I love them so much, there is nothing in the world I would not do for them. I just want to draw them up in my arms and hug them all the time. It's easy to believe God loves little children because they are so sweet and pure.

Then we think about the saints of old, some who have gone on to be with the Lord and some who are still serving Him. We may think of the great generals of faith, those who have given their lives on foreign soil in the mission field, or even a saintly old relative. Of course God loves them! They have walked through trials, pioneered trails of faith and revelation, and spent hours on their knees in prayer. They stood faithful for decades of time, so certainly God loves them.

It's even easier to see how God would love poor and struggling unbelievers, who don't know any better, than it is to see how He could love me. I can understand His compassion for the sinner trapped in bondage without any knowledge of God, but I'm a Christian and I'm supposed to know better and act better than they do. I'm supposed to do everything right, or at least walk in the truth I know. But I miss it from time to time— and sometimes I miss it big time! I know all my faults and weaknesses. It doesn't seem possible that God could love me as much as He loves the ones I think are worthy of His love—like innocent children, great ministers, godly Christians, or even ignorant unbelievers.

The Bible tells us this is wrong thinking!

We dare not make ourselves of the number, or compare ourselves with some that commend themselves: but they measuring themselves by themselves, and comparing themselves among themselves, are not wise.

2 Corinthians 10:12

Don't be a fool and compare yourself with others! You are who God created you to be, and He loves YOU. You must stop believing this lie of the enemy that you have not done enough and are not good enough, faithful enough, or wise enough for God's love. *God's love for you is not based on your character or performance. His love for you is based upon His character and performance,* which is LOVE. He cannot help Himself! He loves you because that is the way He is and that is the relationship He has chosen to have with you. *You are His child.* He loves you more than you love your children. His love passes your human understanding because God is *pure love.*

Believe the Truth

You must fully embrace God's love for you because it is *truth.* It is what God says in His Word. You can read this truth in the Ephesians 3 prayer and numerous other Scripture verses. When you believe these truths, you will have powerful, productive faith. It is easy to trust God and His Word when you understand, accept, and live your life according to His love for you.

There's something revolutionary about believing that nothing you can do will change God's love for you, that you can't stop Him from loving you. You can do things that don't please Him, that don't bring honor to Him, and that may not reflect on Him very well, but there is *nothing* you can do to stop Him from loving you. You are His child and He chooses to love you unconditionally. Knowing this gives you faith to believe His Word concerning miracles and healing and prosperity. It also gives you an overwhelming desire and supernatural strength to please Him and defeat sin in your life.

Believe the truth! God loves you unconditionally. He is the perfect parent, and you are His child. You have all the rights and privileges of a beloved son or daughter of God. You are blessed! You will walk in those rights and privileges and blessings if you simply believe He loves you as His beloved child.

CHAPTER 2

A Heart of Love

When you know God's love for you and your love for Him is the inspiration and motivation for all you think, say, and do—your heart is completely His. The Bible equates the heart with the soil from which everything in your life grows. In Ephesians 3:17 we read that you are to be rooted and grounded in love. God wants your roots to be planted in soil that is love because love is the soil in which faith can flourish, stand strong through every trial and trouble, and produce great fruit.

Any farmer will tell you that the quality of the soil determines the flavor of the crop or fruit that is grown in it. In the state of Georgia, they have soil that produces peaches that are famous for their flavor and sweetness. There are peach parks in that state where you can buy some of the best peaches in the world. I realize there are many places where peaches are grown, but Georgia peaches are world famous because the soil produces a great tasting peach.

If you like tomatoes, you may be aware that all tomatoes are not the same. There's a place in Alabama called Sand Mountain, and if you've ever had a Sand Mountain tomato, you'll throw rocks at all the others! Why? The ground imparts a particularly good flavor to the tomatoes.

When I was in the Fiji Islands, I met a man who had developed hydroponic vegetables. He gave us a tour of the island and asked me, "Do you like corn?"

I said, "Oh yeah! I love corn."

He proceeded to go over to the cornfield and break an ear of corn off a cornstalk. Then he broke it in two, giving half to my wife and half to me, saying, "Try that."

I thought, *You must be crazy. I've eaten raw corn before, and I prefer boiled corn with some butter and salt on it!* But I wanted to be a good guest, so I went along and bit into it. It was like eating boiled corn! It was so tender and sweet. I never tasted anything like it in all my life. How could that be? The nutrient solution it was growing in gave it a fantastic flavor and tender consistency.

Spiritually, the soil of our hearts produces the flavor and consistency of our lives. The fruit we produce is the direct result of the condition of the soil of our hearts. That's why God wants us to be rooted and grounded in love. He wants the soil of our hearts to have the character of love so that everything we say and do in faith reflects Him, for God is love.

Jesus talked about the difference the quality of the soil makes when He explained the parable of the sower in Mark 4:13-20. He began by saying that if we don't understand the parable of the sower, then we will not understand His other parables. He said that the seed of God's Word is sown in different types of ground. Soil that was stony, contained thorns, or was by the wayside would not produce. However, good ground would produce a harvest. The soil represented the heart of the believer.

Jesus wants believers to understand that the parable of the sower deals with the condition of our hearts when we receive the Word of God, which is probably the most fundamental, vital part of our faith. Jesus made it clear that our hearts must be good ground to receive the seed of God's Word and bear good fruit, so what constitutes "good ground"? The answer is in Ephesians 3:17. Our hearts are good ground when we are rooted and grounded in *agape*, God's unconditional love.

According to 1 Corinthians 13:8, love never fails, and Galatians 5:6 says that faith works by love. Therefore, your faith can fail if it is not rooted and grounded in the understanding of God's love for you.

Keeping Your Faith From Failing

The Lord said, Simon, Simon, behold, Satan hath desired to have you, that he may sift you as wheat:

But I have prayed for thee, that thy faith fail not: and when thou art converted, strengthen thy brethren.

Luke 22:31-32

Many times through the years as I looked at this passage of Scripture, I was puzzled by something. I said to the Lord, "Obviously, You are telling believers that it is possible for our faith to fail because You told Peter You would pray that his faith would fail *not*. If my faith can fail, I need to know what that point of failure is! I've based my whole life on faith in You, and I don't want my faith in You and Your Word to fail."

We know the Word can't fail, but if our faith can fail, then where can it fail? How can it fail? Remember that our faith has to be rooted and grounded first and foremost in the revelation of the love of God for us personally. We have to experience it for ourselves. It has to be real in our hearts and minds. This is extremely important because without experiencing God's love personally, it's easy to think that the Word applies to everyone else but me. We cannot embrace and have faith in God's Word to be performed in our lives without knowing He loves us.

The Bible tells us clearly that the Word of God will never fail. If you believe His Word for salvation—you have faith in Jesus Christ as your Lord and Savior, have believed God raised Him from the dead, and have confessed Him as your Lord—then you are definitely born again. You are saved. You are certain of this because the Word of God is true and stands forever. (Matthew 24:35.)

Obviously, your faith didn't fail when you got saved. When you heard that God loves you just the way you are, flawed and imperfect, you suddenly had faith for salvation. But now that you're saved, what about healing? What about the finances you need? What about the family problems that need to be resolved? What about your dreams and calling? Can your faith fail in these issues?

I live in Alabama, and in this state we have thunderstorms, occasional tornadoes, and down on the Gulf Coast a hurricane sometimes blows in. These storms produce a lot of wind! But we also have huge oak trees that have been here for over a hundred years. They've got big branches and their root systems are as large and deep below the surface as the branches above are big and tall. One day after a big storm I drove down a road in my hometown and passed a tree I've passed many times. It had been a part of my life. But that day when I passed by, it was lying uprooted in the front yard of somebody's house, and yet the tree was still intact. None of the branches were broken, and the root system was all there. It was lying next to a huge hole in the ground where the roots had been.

That showed me a perfect illustration of what Jesus was talking about when He prayed for Peter "that your faith fail not." The tree (God's Word) didn't fail. What gave way was the ground (heart) it was planted in. The ground it was planted in was not strong enough to hold the tree against the resistance of that storm. The soil gave way because it was not firm enough to hold out.

The soil of your heart is where the roots of faith grow, and it has to be firmly established in God's love. If the seed of the Word of God is planted in anything other than a heart filled with God's love for YOU, then when the storms of life blow and the pressure gets intense, your faith can fail—that is, your heart will give up and let go. The Word will stand true, but if your belief in it is based on anything other than God's love for you, your faith can be uprooted. His love for you is the only thing that will keep your roots intact and your faith from failing. A heart established in His love is the soil that will hold faith firmly through any storm.

This truth will totally transform your life. It will make the soil of your heart the flavor and consistency of love—God's love for you and your love for Him. Then your faith will not fail during storms and trials, and your life will produce remarkable fruit. The people around you will taste and see that the Lord is good because you move in miracle-working faith that is rooted and grounded in a heart of love.

Who Is the Disciple Whom Jesus Loves?

We are going to look at a progression of Scriptures in the Gospel of John that will reveal a great truth from God's Word about having a heart of love. If you have never seen this before, I guarantee that you will never be the same! We will begin with

Jesus and the disciples at the Last Supper. The Bible says that leaning on Jesus' bosom was the disciple "whom Jesus loved."

> *Now there was leaning on Jesus' bosom one of his disciples, whom Jesus loved.*
>
> John 13:23

Later, after Jesus had been tried, convicted, and sentenced, we see Him hanging on the Cross. The following verses of Scripture also name a particular disciple whom Jesus loved.

> *When Jesus therefore saw his mother, and the disciple standing by, whom he loved, he saith unto his mother, Woman, behold thy son! Then saith he to the disciple, Behold thy mother! And from that hour that disciple took her unto his own home.*
>
> John 19:26-27

Next we visit the time after Jesus died and had been placed in the tomb. It was the first day of the week, resurrection Sunday. Again, we read about this disciple who is described as the disciple whom Jesus loved.

> *The first day of the week cometh Mary Magdalene early, when it was yet dark, unto the sepulchre, and seeth the stone taken away from the sepulchre.*
> *Then she runneth, and cometh to Simon Peter, and to the other disciple, whom Jesus loved, and saith unto them, They have taken away the Lord out of the sepulchre, and we know not where they have laid him.*
>
> John 20:1-2

Finally, we look at the time after Jesus was resurrected and appeared to His disciples on the beach. They had been fishing all night and had caught nothing. Jesus was on the beach and called out to them to cast their net on the other side of their boat. When they did, the catch of fish was so large, their net broke. Realizing this had happened before with Jesus, the disciple who recognized Jesus was also the disciple whom Jesus loved.

> *Therefore that disciple whom Jesus loved saith unto Peter, It is the Lord. Now when Simon Peter heard that it was the Lord, he girt his fisher's coat unto him, (for he was naked,) and did cast himself into the sea.*

> John 21:7

Who is this disciple whom Jesus loved? At the end of John's Gospel, we find out.

> *This is the disciple which testifieth of these things, and wrote these things: and we know that his testimony is true.*

> John 21:24

The disciple whom Jesus loved is the Apostle John, the author of the Book of John. I think it's interesting that he refers to himself in the third person. John does not say, "*I* leaned on Jesus at the Last Supper, *I* was the one He gave His mother to when He was on the Cross, and Peter and *I* were the first to hear about the empty tomb from Mary Magdalene." Instead of giving his name, he just calls himself "the disciple whom Jesus loved."

This sounds a little arrogant at first, but what we discover is that John had a powerful revelation of the fact that he was the object and target of God's love. If you want to be on fire for God, walking in extreme faith, you need to know that you are the object and target of God's love. You must believe that if God loves anybody, He loves YOU.

The truth is, if John called himself the disciple whom Jesus loved, then you and I can call ourselves the same thing. And we must remember that the Holy Spirit inspired John to speak of himself this way. That is because God wants each of His children to call themselves "the disciple whom Jesus loves." The Bible says that God is no respecter of persons. (Romans 2:11.) His Word is true for everyone. He loves everyone with the same pure, unconditional love. John just got the revelation of God's love for him before the rest of us did.

Who is the disciple Jesus loves?

YOU are the disciple whom Jesus loves!

Any child of God can boldly proclaim, "I am the disciple whom Jesus loves!"

Confidence and Divine Protection

Let's look at this in another light. In John, chapter 21, Jesus spoke about future events, including the death of the disciple whom He loved.

Verily, verily, I say unto thee, When thou wast young, thou gird-
edst thyself, and walkedst whither thou wouldest: but when thou
shalt be old, thou shalt stretch forth thy hands, and another shall
gird thee, and carry thee whither thou wouldest not.

This spake he, signifying by what death he should glorify God. And
when he had spoken this, he saith unto him, Follow me.

Then Peter, turning about, seeth the disciple whom Jesus loved
following; which also leaned on his breast at supper, and said,
Lord, which is he that betrayeth thee?

Peter seeing him saith to Jesus, Lord, and what shall this man do?
Jesus saith unto him, If I will that he tarry till I come, what is that
to thee? follow thou me.

Then went this saying abroad among the brethren, that that disci-
ple should not die: yet Jesus said not unto him, He shall not die;
but, If I will that he tarry till I come, what is that to thee?

John 21:18-23

In this passage of Scripture, Jesus indicated that Peter was going to die in a way that he would not wish to die, but John would die of natural causes. Could it be that because John had a revelation of Jesus' love for him, he knew God's supernatural power would keep him safe from all harm and sickness?

The Bible tells us very little about how the Apostles died. In Acts 12:2 it says that James was beheaded, but most of what we know comes from church history and tradition. The early church fell under great persecution and many were crucified like Jesus. Church history tells us that Peter insisted on being crucified upside down because he did not feel worthy to be crucified in the same manner Jesus had been crucified.

Of the eleven Apostles remaining after Judas hanged himself, each suffered a martyr's death—all except the Apostle John. Church history tells us that they tried to kill him by boiling him in oil, but he refused to die. Because they couldn't kill him, John was exiled to a prison island, a little place called Patmos.[1] It was there that he wrote the Book of Revelation, revealing our resurrected Lord Jesus and the future of the church and the earth.

What was it that singled John out and kept him alive? Why didn't he die in the boiling oil? Why did the Lord give the Book of Revelation to us through him? I'm convinced it was because John had a revelation of God's love for him. He fully accepted his position as the disciple whom Jesus loved, and when you know you are the object of God's love, you know there is no end to the revelation and supernatural protection He provides you.

You also know that anyone or anything that crosses you is crossing God! Those who oppose God usually end up at the bottom of the Red Sea or under the walls of Jericho. And those who love God and know His love for them will live out their lives in His divine protection. Obviously, it is a good thing to know God's love! There is nothing like it.

When you really know the love of Jesus Christ, practically and through experience, it will make you bulletproof. Your heart is so full of God's love for you that you will have a solid confidence and faith in His divine protection. You don't have to worry about anything!

Knowing His love will cause you to be in the right place at the right time, and you can avoid catastrophe, calamity, and tragedy. He will direct your steps, light your path, and show you things to come. Though a thousand fall at your side, and ten thousand at your right hand, it shall not come near you! (Psalm 91:7.)

CHAPTER 3

The Difference Love Makes

My mother had a hallway that ran through the middle of her house, and in that hallway she had pictures of various people, mostly of our family. Every one of those pictures was of someone she loved, those who were important to her. I'd walk past them and see my high school picture, where I looked nerdy and goofy, and my childhood pictures when my hair was buzzed, and I'd think, *Oh man, I wish she'd take these pictures down!* But you know what? Even though I didn't like those particular pictures of me, the fact that she had them hanging on her wall gave me an inner security that she loved me unconditionally, that she saw something special and loveable in me.

God wants you to know that your picture is hanging on His wall, and He carries your picture in His wallet. He knows you inside and out, and He still loves you. You are not lost in a sea of faces in the body-of-Christ picture. He has a special snapshot of you in His heart. He knows your name, He sees your face, He knows where you are, He knows what you're thinking and feeling, and He knows what's going on in your life. He knows what enemies are attacking you. He knows what targets the devil has painted on your back. He knows what temptations you are fighting. You are the object of His love, and there's nothing that you can do about it. You can act as ugly as you want to, and it will not change the fact that God loves you.

An Illustration of Love

We can see this kind of unconditional love and loyalty demonstrated in our pets. I'm a soft touch when it comes to animals. We live on an acreage and have six or seven dogs. Two of them are strays, just walk-ups, and they were in bad shape when we gathered them in. I took them to the vet, got them all fixed up and cleaned up, and then moved them into dog paradise—where we live. One of our dogs used to sleep under a bridge, which is where I found him. Now he's got his own little bridge over a stream that goes down into our pond. He is now a bridge owner—and he knows it!

That dog is the smartest of all our dogs. The ones that were store-bought or have been raised in this lifestyle of luxury are likely to go anywhere and do anything. They could be in the street, across the road, or off exploring for a while and then come back. But the dog I found under the bridge stays close to home. From the day I opened the passenger door to my pickup truck and he jumped in and laid his chin on my knee, he's hardly left my side. I see him watching those other dogs running in different directions, and he'll look up at me like he's saying, "Uh-uh, not me. I know where I've got it good. I've been there, I've done that, and I'm not goin' anywhere. I'm stickin' close to you."

That dog has been out there in the world, and he knows what it is to do without. He knows what it means to be lost and homeless, living in poverty, hunger, and loneliness. And he prefers the blessing and prosperity he has with me. If I'm on the property, his eyes are always on me or he's right beside me. His devotion is an illustration of believers who stay in close communion with the Lord at all times because they know there is nothing better than Jesus; He is the source and willing Giver of everything they need or desire in life. They know He takes pleasure in blessing them.

Then we have this other stray dog named Peanut. My daughter actually had to lure her in. She slept in the woods across the street, and we started leaving food out for her. She would eat the food, but we never could get close to her. Finally one day she came close enough for us to touch her, and after she warmed up to us a little, we took her to the vet. The vet cleaned her up and got her healthy, and then we took her to live with us.

It soon became obvious that Peanut had been abused, and although she's been a part of the Webb zoo for several years now, she still can't stand much attention. If you reach out to touch her, she immediately cowers like she thinks you're going to hit her. Knowing how she is and that she needs tender, loving care, I've never even raised my voice to her, but she still cowers.

One day I was walking out the front door when Peanut was lying on the porch. I said, "Hello, Peanut," and I reached out to scratch her behind the ears. As always, she drew back when I reached out to her. I looked at her and said, "Peanut, I don't know what else I can do to convince you it's okay. I wish you'd just go ahead and act like you belong here."

When I said that the Holy Ghost spoke to me on the inside, "Yeah, I wish that for a lot of My people. I wish My children would act like they belong in My presence. Every time I reach out to them, they think I'm going to slap them down when I just want to bless them."

Every good gift and every perfect gift is from above, and cometh down from the Father of lights, with whom is no variableness, neither shadow of turning.

James 1:17

Everything God has in His hand for us is good. Every time He reaches in our direction, He's reaching out to give us something good, to bless us, to do good for us. But if we have been hurt and abused by our own parents, other relatives, friends, teachers, or neighbors, we have a hard time accepting the fact that we are the object of God's love. Instead of having the peace and security of knowing He has our picture hanging on His wall, we think He wants our heads hanging on His wall!

We need to be assured that God loves us even more than a mother who glances at our picture every time she goes down the hall. And we need to be like our dog from under the bridge, who just accepts that he's been fully saved by his master who loves him. We must see ourselves as beloved citizens of Heaven and children of God. And as we stay close to our Master, we joyfully receive every benefit and blessing that comes with that position.

When we see how much God loves us, we see ourselves and our lives in a completely different light. We are no longer like Peanut, cowering and afraid of everything and everybody—especially our master. God's love transforms our lives so that we can be confident and peaceful at all times.

Believers who don't know God's love for them never fully understand the power of their right standing with Him. Therefore, they don't know how to properly deal with temptation and sin. As a result, they either eventually give up trying to live godly lives and live like the devil, or they become so uptight and religious—certain that at the slightest mistake God will strike them with lightning—that their lives are more like hell than Heaven. Their faith is ineffective and their lives are a mess because they don't know God's love.

One of the greatest differences an understanding of the love of God makes in a believer's life is the ability to overcome sin.

You see, faith is not just for miracles and healing and financial prosperity. Primarily, our faith in God gives us the strength to resist temptation and deal with any sin, fault, or weakness in our lives. When our minds and hearts are free from the guilt of sin, there is no way the enemy can bring us into condemnation; and when we are free from condemnation, we can easily have faith in God to move in our behalf.

Love Forgives and Restores

Just like my dog that stays close to me and never wants to do anything but love me and please me, the revelation that God loves YOU changes your whole perspective on sin. You just don't want to sin anymore! You just want to be with Jesus and please Him. When temptation comes, the knowledge of His love for you and your love for Him rises up in you to resist that temptation and walk away. And, knowing He loves you will also cause you to respond in the right way if you do sin or miss it. The Holy Spirit convicts you of your sin, and at the same time His love calls you back into fellowship with Him. Then you can repent, receive forgiveness, and continue walking with Him in complete faith because you have a clear conscience.

First John 1:9 states, "If we confess our sins, he is faithful and just to forgive us our sins, and to cleanse us from all unrighteousness." God is telling us how to get back on track with Him when we miss it. He loves us just as much when we have failed and disappointed Him as when we are walking upright and in right standing with Him. However, He also knows how the enemy works on you when you sin. The devil will condemn you and take away your hope and confidence if you have sinned, so God tells you that He will always forgive you, cleanse you, and restore you because He is a just and good God. All you have to do is to turn to Him and repent, confessing that you messed up, and receive His love and forgiveness.

If you don't respond to the conviction of the Holy Spirit and act on 1 John 1:9 to receive forgiveness and cleansing, you will come under the devil's condemnation. Then shame and self-hatred will set in. Satan's condemnation always causes people to despise themselves and take it out on others; God's love and forgiveness will always cause people to love themselves and have compassion on others, and that will keep their faith strong. First John 1:9 was written to keep you from the enemy's influence and bondage. It will keep your heart established in God's love and forgiveness so that your faith will remain effective at all times.

Can you see what a monumental difference a revelation of the love of God makes when it comes to living your Christian life? Knowing God loves you is the basis for walking in the Spirit and not fulfilling the lusts of your flesh. The Bible says in Galatians 5:16 that walking in the Spirit is the key to overcoming your flesh, the temptations of this world, and everything the devil throws at you to tempt you to sin. Furthermore, you can rest in the knowledge that even if you do miss it, God will always forgive you, cleanse you, and put your feet back on the right path. Why? Because He loves you!

In Luke 22:31-34, Jesus said that Satan's desire was to sift Peter as wheat, and that He prayed for Peter, that his faith would not fail. He went on to tell Peter that he would be tempted and would deny Him three times. Peter stated he would go with Jesus to prison or even to death. Later, in Luke 22:55-62, three times Satan tempted Peter to deny Jesus, and three times Peter yielded, saying, "No, I don't know Him." After that, Peter ran away, weeping bitterly. How do you think he was feeling? Can you see how he might have thought, *I've let Jesus down when He needed me most, and there's no way that He could ever forgive me, that He could ever say, "Peter, I forgive you. Just forget it."*

We know Satan tormented Peter over this. He was the one who tempted Peter to deny Jesus in the first place, and then he condemned him for doing it! But what did Jesus do? True to His nature, He demonstrated His great love and forgiveness. Not only had He told Peter that He was praying for him before this happened, but after He was resurrected He told the women at the tomb to go to the disciples AND Peter, naming Peter person-ally. Later, when Jesus walked with Peter along the seashore, He confirmed His unconditional love for Peter by giving him three opportunities to affirm his love. He told Peter, "If you love Me, feed My sheep." Jesus was reestablishing Peter's heart in love so that his faith would not fail. And Jesus wants to do the same thing for anyone who sins or makes a mistake.

Just because you sin or make a mistake does not mean your faith has failed; providing, of course, that you are restored as Peter was by repenting, receiving forgiveness, and believing he was forgiven. Jesus loves you as much as He loved Peter *even after he denied Him*. Peter's failures did not change Jesus' love for him!

Three times Jesus gave Peter the opportunity to affirm his love for Him by asking if he loved Him more than "these." Jesus was asking, "Peter, do you love Me, really love Me? If you do, then you'll know I have a plan for your life, and it is bigger than fishing with your buddies. If you do, you'll be willing to do what I've called you to do."

Jesus questioned Peter, and the first two times Peter answered, "Yea, Lord; thou knowest that I love thee" (John 21:15-16). The third time Peter was grieved and answered, "Lord, thou knowest all things; thou knowest that I love thee."

Jesus looked at Peter and told him, "Feed My lambs. Feed My sheep." By speaking those words, Jesus was telling Peter, "You are forgiven, and your failure is forgotten. I know you love Me because I love you and have put My love in you. Now go out and start doing what I've called you to do. Preach and teach My Word to My people."

When you know that God loves you, your faith will take root in ground that cannot give way, even if you fail Him. Like Peter, you can know that His love can restore you from any transgression and keep your dreams from dying and your vision from waning. Knowing He loves you preserves your dreams and your hope!

The devil's mission is to kill dreams and hope. He is trying to stop your vision from coming to pass by tempting you to sin, and then condemning you if you do. He wants to destroy your faith in God by lying and trying to convince you that if you miss it, God does not love you enough to forgive you, to continue to bless you, and to see all your dreams fulfilled. This is how the devil operates; he is a thief and a liar.

When the devil brings that kind of thought to me, telling me, "You've really done it this time—God's had it with you, and there's no way He'll forgive you this time," how do I know it is a lie? The Bible tells me so! Jesus restored Peter and immediately put him to work. He told Peter that he was forgiven, his sin was forgotten, and now he needed to get busy about the business of fishing for men and feeding the sheep. Jesus saw to it that Peter's gifts and calling were fulfilled. And what Jesus did for Peter He'll do for you and me and anyone who repents!

Too many Christians get under condemnation if they sin or know they have not pleased God. Because they don't know God's unconditional love for them, condemnation will rule them and they stop going to church, serving the Lord, and fulfilling His call on their lives. They have no faith to believe He will forgive them and restore them to fellowship with Him. That's why it is so important to know and live in His love. God's love doesn't fail even when we do—and that makes a tremendous difference in our lives!

The Delight of His Love

Delight thyself also in the LORD: and he shall give thee the desires of thine heart.

Psalm 37:4

A wonderful thing happens when you fall so in love with the Lord that He is all you want or need: He can fulfill your dreams and give you the desires of your heart. He knows He's number one in your life and your love for Him is so great that nothing else satisfies. All you want to do is spend time with Him, getting to know him, and fulfilling His will for your life. You cringe at the thought of sinning or grieving Him in any way. And without Him, any gifts, blessings, favor, or honor are nothing to you. Jesus is everything!

When you delight yourself in the Lord by understanding, accepting, and surrendering your whole heart to the love He has for you, He joyfully gives you the desires of your heart. His love and protection can preserve your life. Not only do you have a joyous life, but you also have a productive life, filled with His presence. For all these reasons we can say that the difference the love of God makes in our everyday lives is beyond measure!

CHAPTER 4

Knowing God

God's love is the basis of our faith in Him, and our faith in Him is the key to a productive, fulfilled life. Without faith our lives are empty and the devil will run right over us. Therefore, we must walk in love for our faith to stand strong and our lives to be all God ordained them to be. But how do we get that deep revelation of God's love for us?

> *Beloved, let us love one another: for love is of God; and every one that loveth is born of God, and knoweth God.*
> *He that loveth not knoweth not God; for God is love.*
>
> 1 John 4:7-8

This passage tells us very plainly that only those who are born of God AND KNOW GOD can truly love. Verse 8 says those who do not love do not really *know* God because God is love. But it doesn't say that they are not born of God. A person can be born of God and not know God, which means you can be born again and not walk in love. Only those who truly love are both born of God and know God. The Word is teaching us that because faith works by love, and true love comes only by knowing God, *we need to know God!*

What do you really know about God? You can have faith only in someone you know well enough to trust, someone you have had a significant amount of experience with to know how they generally think, speak, and act in various situations. Do you know God that well?

I see many Christians who know a lot of Scriptures about faith, but they never seem to walk in victory or mature spiritually. I've come to the conclusion that, to a great extent, it's because they don't really know God. They can quote verses like, "God is love," and especially John 10:10, "I am come that they might have life, and that they might have it more abundantly." But they have never really taken the time to dig into the Word and let the Holy Spirit reveal how God thinks, what He feels about various things, and what He expects from them. People need to know what God's desire is for them to be and do in life.

If I treated my relationship with my wife the way most believers treat their relationship with God, I would be in big trouble! But through the years I have made it a priority to get to know her, and today I believe I do know her better than anyone else on this earth. I have a love relationship with her that goes back more than thirty-five years. I don't stay faithful to her because I'm afraid of what she'll do to me! I stay faithful to her because I love her and she loves me. Sometimes I'm amazed at how she loves me, because I know me and I'm probably not the easiest person to live with; but you'd never know it from her.

I know my wife loves me and I can trust her. If she tells me she's going to meet me at a certain restaurant and buy my lunch at noon, I know she will do it. How do I know she's telling me the truth? She's not going to lie to me because she loves me. I have total confidence in her. She would never lie to me or do anything to hurt me.

The same holds true for my relationship with God. I have faith in Him because I have made it a priority to know Him and have experienced His love for me. Over the years His love for me has reinforced and strengthened my faith in Him, and I have seen Him do amazing, miraculous things. The Holy Spirit has taught me from His Word what He likes and doesn't like and what He expects from me as His son. Many times He has spoken to me to say and do things that required me to exercise my faith in Him, and now He and I have a track record that makes my faith bold in the face of any trouble or challenge.

Bold Faith

Herein is our love made perfect, that we may have boldness in the day of judgment: because as he is, so are we in this world.

1 John 4:17

When God's love is made perfect, it has matured in our hearts and has developed such confidence in us that we become bold. We have such bold faith that we don't even worry about the Day of Judgment! Our eternal future is already settled, and we can approach that day with a holy confidence. But this verse is also talking about being bold in the everyday trials of life. The Greek word translated "judgment" is *krisis*, where we get our English word "crisis."[1]

From time to time everyone will experience a crisis. What do we do when crisis confronts us? What is our bold response? We can respond with 1 John 4:17 and say, "My love has been made perfect, so I boldly say today to this crisis that as Jesus is, so am I right now in this world. I am in Him and He is not doing without so I am not doing without. Mountain, get out of my life!"

When a crisis such as sickness, family problems, or a mountain of debt comes, we can have bold faith to declare our healing, wisdom, and deliverance. Instead of caving in and becoming an emotional wreck, we can be like Jesus. We can draw on God's strength and courage to speak boldly to that crisis. Why do we have such boldness? Like Jesus, we know God loves us and wants us to overcome and obtain victory in every crisis of life.

For verily I say unto you, That whosoever shall say unto this mountain, Be thou removed, and be thou cast into the sea; and shall

not doubt in his heart, but shall believe that those things which he
saith shall come to pass; he shall have whatsoever he saith.
Therefore I say unto you, What things soever ye desire, when ye
pray, believe that ye receive them, and ye shall have them.

Mark 11:23-24

Because God loves me, He wrote Mark 11:23-24 to ME. I
know that as I believe and act upon His Word to me, it is going
to work for me. Jesus said, "That whosoever...," and I'm that
"whosoever." He was talking to me! I can say to that mountain
of sickness, family problems, or debt, "Crisis, be removed and
cast into the sea," and that crisis will move. It won't move
because I'm such a great person; it will move because I have
bold faith in my God, whom I have come to know so well. I
know He delights in me, and I believe His promises to me. I am
the disciple whom He loves. I am His beloved son, and sin no
longer divides us. This kind of confidence in the love of God,
this kind of bold faith, comes from constant fellowship and
communion with the Father, as we live in His presence and
abide in His Word.

Love is made perfect in the continual presence of the Lord,
getting to know Him by the Word and the Spirit.

When I see cherished ministry friends or relatives that I
haven't been around for a while or had regular communication
with, it may take some time for us to relax or feel comfortable
and easy with one another again. That's not true with my relationship with my wife. I communicate with her all the time,

even when we are not together, so when we are together there is no stiffness or timidity. We are just easy with one another.

In the same way, if you are fellowshipping with the Father every day—spending special time with Him, reading the Word and meditating on His promises—you will keep that closeness and maintain your confidence. Then, when a crisis arises, you can have boldness to speak His Word into that situation and know that everything is going to be all right.

> *When thou passest through the waters, I will be with thee; and through the rivers, they shall not overflow thee: when thou walkest through the fire, thou shalt not be burned; neither shall the flame kindle upon thee.*
>
> Isaiah 43:2

Knowing God and being established in His love for you will make you *bold*. You can be like Shadrach, Meshach, and Abednego, whose story is told in Daniel, chapter 3. When King Nebuchadnezzar issued the decree, "Bow to me or burn," these three men boldly held their position of faith in God and defied the king's command. This promise of God in Isaiah 43:2 assured them that if they went through fire, God would be with them and they would not be burned. The flame would not even ignite their clothing!

Without hesitation Shadrach, Meshach, and Abednego told the king, "Hear our answer, O King. If your plan won't accommodate our devotion to our God, just go ahead and heat up the furnace. We are not going to bow to your image, and our God will deliver us out of your hand."

King Nebuchadnezzar got so mad, he added more fuel to the fire and had his mightiest men tie them up and cast them into the burning furnace. The fire was so hot that it killed the men who threw them in! But when the king looked into the furnace, he saw four men loose, walking in the midst of the fire, and the Bible says they suffered no hurt. Jesus went to Shadrach, Meshach, and Abednego in the fire, and when Jesus is with you in the furnace or in the office or in the car, things are going to be okay!

Even though these men of God went through the fire, they suffered no harm. The Bible states in Daniel 3:27, "...these men, upon whose bodies the fire had no power, nor was an hair of their head singed, neither were their coats changed, nor the smell of fire had passed on them." These three Hebrew men demonstrated faith and confidence that God would deliver them based on His Word and His love for them.

A heart full of God's love is open to hear His voice and act on His Word because you have complete confidence and faith in Him. Responding to His voice will cause you to be in the right place at the right time. He will direct your steps, light your path, and show you things to come. Because God loves you, He protects you, as any parent would protect their child whom they dearly love.

Having a heart of love secures the Word of God in your life and makes your faith bold and unshakable!

Knowing Him Defines You

When you get to know your natural parents, you understand yourself better. They let you know what is yours and what is not yours, what your natural abilities and talents are, what pleases them, and what is expected of you. The same is true with your Heavenly Father. As you get to know Him, you see more and more who you are and what your purpose is.

Your Heavenly Father tells you that as His child you are not only accepted as part of the family of God, but you are accepted as an *equal* part of the family. You are not only *equal* with your brothers and sisters in Christ, but also you are *equal* with Jesus. Now before you cry, "Heresy!" let me explain. You are not God like He is, nor do you hold His position as Head of the Church, but you are His joint-heir. What He inherited through His death and resurrection, you also inherited.

> *If children, then heirs; heirs of God, and joint-heirs with Christ; if so be that we suffer with him, that we may be also glorified together.*
>
> Romans 8:17

You are in Him and God loves you just as much as He loves Jesus. That is what Jesus prayed in John, chapter 17, and Jesus always prays the perfect will of the Father.

Neither pray I for these alone, but for them also which shall believe on me through their word;

That they all may be one; as thou, Father, art in me, and I in thee, that they also may be one in us: that the world may believe that thou hast sent me.

And the glory which thou gavest me I have given them; that they may be one, even as we are one:

I in them, and thou in me, that they may be made perfect in one; and that the world may know that thou hast sent me, and hast loved them, as thou hast loved me.

And I have declared unto them thy name, and will declare it: that the love wherewith thou hast loved me may be in them, and I in them.

John 17:20-23,26

Most of what you will have in this life will come through your faith in what God says in His Word. By knowing Him and His Word you learn your rights, privileges, and blessings as a joint-heir with Jesus. You also grow in the revelation of who you are as a son or daughter of God.

Behold, what manner of love the Father hath bestowed upon us, that we should be called the sons of God.

1 John 3:1

This is a good verse to confess over yourself. Saying confidently that God loves you so much that He accepted you as His child not only gives you a revelation of God's love for you, but it develops your understanding of who you are in Him, what is expected of you as His son or daughter, and what you have in Him.

God has given you rights and privileges as a joint-heir with Christ Jesus! Get to know Him, and continue in your relationship to know Him more deeply. You will experience more and more of His love in your heart and more and more of His power in your life.

CHAPTER 5

Joint-Heirs Have Ownership

The Spirit itself beareth witness with our spirit, that we are the children of God:

And if children, then heirs; heirs of God, and joint-heirs with Christ; if so be that we suffer with him, that we may be also glorified together.

Romans 8:16-17

Once your faith is firmly established in your personal love relationship with God and you begin to identify yourself first and foremost as His beloved son or daughter, you need to learn what is legally and rightfully yours in Jesus Christ. When you were born again and became part of the family of God, you were granted ownership of certain things. The Bible declares that you are a joint-heir with Jesus, and what He inherited, you inherited.

As God's child you have an inheritance that He wants you to have. Be sure you understand this important fact: *God wants you to have everything that belongs to you!* Certainly He doesn't need it, and He paid a great price for you to have it. That alone should be enough motivation for you to find out what is yours, how to possess it, and for what purposes He wants you to use it.

God's Last Will and Testament

Often you hear people refer to "the will of God," when talking about the circumstances and situations of life that are affecting them. Most of the time they really mean "the whim of God" because they are referring to some unexpected thing that happened. They believe everything that happens, good or bad, must be God's will, even though there is no reason to attribute the event to God.

People are often so ignorant of God's Word, which clearly is His will, that they implicate God and His will in random things that He had nothing to do with. They don't believe God honors His Word, that He will do what He said He will do, or that the laws He set in motion to rule the universe are still at work. They must think God just makes things up as He goes along, doing everything on a whim. But the Bible doesn't give any evidence of God doing anything by whim or impulse. The Bible is God's *will*, and a will is a legal document. Legally, God has bound His will with His Word.

When someone dies, their will defines what they desire to happen in their absence. Their beneficiaries will receive whatever is decreed in the deceased person's last will and testament. The will states to whom their worldly possessions are to go. In most cases, if there is no surviving spouse, everything would be divided among the children.

God is our Father, and we are His children. We are the children whom Jesus died to save and restore to the Father. We are the family God wanted when He made Adam and Eve in the Garden of Eden. Think about this. Jesus died and rose again to save us. When we were born again, our old sin nature died and our spirits were made alive to God, receiving His righteousness. According to 2 Corinthians 5:17, when we were born again we became new creatures, a brand-new species of beings that never existed before. Our spirits were made new and we were no longer separated from God by our sin but were accepted by Him and made a part of His family. It doesn't get any better than that!

> *God, who is rich in mercy, for his great love wherewith he loved us,*
> *Even when we were dead in sins, hath quickened us together with Christ, (by grace ye are saved;)*
> *And hath raised us up together, and made us sit together in heavenly places in Christ Jesus:*
> *That in the ages to come he might shew the exceeding riches of his grace in his kindness toward us through Christ Jesus.*
>
> Ephesians 2:4-7

If I accept who I now am in Christ Jesus, then I also realize the responsibility that goes with the position I have received. If

I am sitting with Him in heavenly places, ruling and reigning with Him, I am not supposed to be just sitting and doing nothing. Jesus said that the greatest among men is one who is servant to others (Matthew 23:11), so I need to be serving Him with all my heart, soul, and strength.

To serve God effectively, however, I must know His will for my life. I need to know who I am in Him, but then I also need to know what He wants me to have. What did He leave for me in the will? I must read the will to find out, and God's will is the Holy Bible.

The Bible, the written Word of God, is a legal document that no human being or devil can change. His will cannot be changed by contemporary culture, modernism, secularism, humanism, and certainly not by any demonic deception or doctrine. God's will doesn't change with the times and trends of the day. His will is the same because God is the same; He never changes and there is no variableness or turning in Him (Malachi 3:6; James 1:17).

The grass withereth, the flower fadeth: but the word of our God shall stand for ever.

Isaiah 40:8

What the "word of our God" says is mine—*is mine*. The Bible says in Ephesians 2:4-7 that I have been raised up in Jesus and made to sit with Him, ruling and reigning with Him. And, if He wants to spend the rest of my life showing me the exceeding riches of His grace, then that is who I am and what I have. It is the truth regardless of what anyone else thinks about it. It is the truth whether or not I know it and believe it.

Reverend Kenneth Copeland spoke prophetically to me once, saying, "Just go ahead and enjoy it, Son, because it's yours." I heard the Father's voice in those words! Jesus paid for all we would ever need and gave it to us so we would have it and enjoy it. He gave us what we need. You and I are the ones who need power to get wealth so we can establish His covenant in the earth. You and I are the ones who need to be healed and set free to worship and serve Him. You and I are the ones who need all spiritual blessings in Christ Jesus to fulfill His plan for our lives and experience love, joy, and peace.

If God didn't want you to have all of this, He wouldn't have told you how to possess it or have written so much about faith in His Word. But He *does* want you to prosper and be in health even as your soul prospers. (3 John 2.) Your soul (your mind, will, and reasoning abilities) prospers as you read His last will and testament, believe what it says, and possess what it says is yours. Jesus secured His inheritance and yours with His blood, and then He gave you the codebook to teach you how to walk in it and enjoy it. The codebook is the Bible.

In the time we are living, it seems like our culture is obsessed with codes and conspiracies. Popular authors often try to bring the Bible into their strange theories and myths, perhaps to substantiate their philosophy or give their ideas some credibility, authenticity, or validation. But just because someone attaches the term "Bible" or uses references from the Bible in their work does not mean it has anything to do with the Word of God.

It is true that the Bible, God's written, Holy Word, is a codebook. But when you were born again, God put the Decoder inside you. Jesus said He would send the Comforter, the Holy Spirit, whom He also called "the Spirit of truth" (John 15:26), to lead you into all truth. The Holy Spirit came to live in you, teach you, guide you, and empower you. In fact, when you are communing with the Holy Ghost, you are talking with the Author of the Bible himself.

The prophecy came not in old time by the will of man: but holy men of God spake as they were moved by the Holy Ghost.

2 Peter 1:21

The Holy Ghost will teach you all you need to know. He will reveal to you what the Word of God is saying. The One who wrote the last will and testament of Almighty God came to reside in you so He could enable you to know God's will for your life.

Wouldn't it be a shame to get to the end of your life and find out that you had been given millions of dollars, which was gaining interest in an account in your name, but nobody told you about it? And it would be an even bigger shame for you to know that it was yours, that the account was in both your benefactor's name and your name, that you had full access to it, and that it was your benefactor's will for you to use it, but your pride and false piety told you that claiming any of it would be greedy and self-indulgent. Unfortunately, that is the picture of how many believers think today. They either don't know who they are and what they have in Christ, or they do know but their religious ideas and traditions keep them from possessing it and enjoying it.

Your Rights of Ownership

The Bible says, "Faith without works is dead" (James 2:20, 26). It does you no good and certainly does not serve your Heavenly Father well to have bold faith that is rooted and grounded in His love and never use it. In fact, He's given you this inheritance for good reason. As you discover what is yours and use your faith in Him and His Word to possess it, you will become more and more like Jesus and be able to do all He created you to do.

> *Whereby are given unto us exceeding great and precious promises:*
> *that by these ye might be partakers of the divine nature.*
>
> 2 Peter 1:4

We actually partake of God's nature as we exercise our faith in His promises to accomplish His will! But we can do that only if we know our rights of ownership contained in our covenant with God.

Something happened to me years ago that illustrates this. In 1997 my wife saved her money and bought me a brand-new Harley-Davidson Ultra Classic Anniversary Special motorcycle. We were riding a lot in those days, so this was a really great gift. A few years later we were believing God for some other things, and I was looking around for seed to sow. We weren't riding motorcycles much at that time, and I had two of them. I sold one of them, and at first I couldn't see myself selling the one my wife had given me because she had used her faith to get it and it represented her love for me. Then I thought, *That's good, precious seed because it's valuable to me.* So I said, "Lord, I'll sow that if You'll show me where." He told me to sow it to a minister friend of mine, so I gave it to him with no strings attached.

The very next day somebody handed my wife a check for at least equal to but probably more than what the motorcycle would have sold for! We rejoiced over the quick harvest on the seed we had sown, and I didn't think any more about it until later, when I got a series of phone calls about the motorcycle.

In the course of time I learned that the friend I had given the motorcycle to had given it to another man, whom I had never met. That man evidently got involved in something illegal, and I heard he went to prison. Before this he had abandoned the motorcycle in a Wal-Mart parking lot in another state, and the authorities and various other people were calling me because the title was still in my name.

When all this came to light I asked, "Lord, what's going on here?" I was kind of reluctant to get the bike because I had given it away, and when I give something I consider it no longer mine. However, as I prayed I saw something that I hadn't considered. Legally, that motorcycle was mine. The man I had given it to had never transferred ownership. The only legal document attached to it was the title with my name and address on it. Furthermore, no money was ever exchanged on the deal. I had given it to my friend, and he had given me nothing in return. Then he gave it to this other man, who gave him nothing in return.

The more I thought about it, I realized, *You know, that's my motorcycle. The only money that exchanged hands was the money my wife originally paid for it. Otherwise it was just passed around. So legally it's my motorcycle. I own it!*

At that moment I owned the motorcycle, but I did not possess it. So I jumped on a plane to go get my motorcycle. That motorcycle was waiting for me to come get it and bring it back home, and it was just like angels were camped around it. It was dirty but unscratched and unscathed. The next day I arranged for the local Harley store to ship it home to me.

Today that motorcycle is sitting in my basement, where it will remain unless the Lord tells me to do something else with it. I am now both the owner and possessor of it. There was some effort involved to get it, but once I knew that it was legally mine, it was easy to have faith to recover it.

Faith functions in conjunction with ownership, and we come to own something because we either pay for it or receive it as a gift. In the case of our salvation, Jesus paid for it and then He gave it to us. That was His gift to us when we surrendered our lives to Him. As His joint-heir, it behooves us to find out everything we now own in Him.

We cannot have faith to possess something that is not legally ours. God cannot honor our faith if it is not based on what His Word says is ours according to the covenant in Jesus' blood. For example, my wife and I are legally married in the eyes of God. He gave us to each other to be married. Therefore, another man cannot have faith to possess her as his wife because legally she is my wife.

On the other hand, we should be bold to possess that which we know is legally ours in Jesus Christ. Each of us needs to possess what rightfully belongs to us, rising up and saying, "That's mine; it belongs to me and I will not be denied!"

Again, faith operates according to ownership and in the knowledge that we are joint-heirs with Jesus. The value of our salvation is priceless, so we want to use every part of it wisely and glorify Him by knowing and then possessing everything our salvation includes.

Ownership and Possession

There are three possibilities in ownership and possession.

You own something and possess it.

You own something and do not possess it. This means you either have no idea you own it, you know you own it but loaned it to someone else, you know you own it and someone stole it from you, or you know you own it and have not bothered to take the necessary steps to possess it.

You possess something and do not own it. This means you have either borrowed it or stolen it from the owner.

Whichever one of these three applies is determined by what you know is legally yours and whether or not you take steps to possess what is legally yours.

Faith works in conjunction with our rights of ownership, but it does not obtain ownership. Faith causes us to possess what we already own. Ownership, again, is determined by who paid for it, and we did not purchase our salvation. Jesus paid the debt for our sin and purchased our salvation. Then He freely gave it to us. Everything that is ours in this great salvation was given to us—even our faith to get saved.

> *By grace are ye saved through faith; and that not of yourselves: it is the gift of God.*

> Ephesians 2:8

I say, through the grace given unto me, to every man that is among
you, not to think of himself more highly than he ought to think; but
to think soberly, according as God hath dealt to every man the
measure of faith.

Romans 12:3

God gave us the faith to get saved because Jesus purchased our salvation. We did not buy our faith; we received it as a free gift. Now that we have the measure of faith, we must use it to possess what God's Word says we own as joint-heirs with Jesus. As I wrote earlier, it is a sad thing to own something and not possess it.

Years ago I was involved in an incident that demonstrates this point. I was visiting Canaan Land, a Christian facility near Montgomery, Alabama, which is a ministry that provides housing and help for men who have been involved with drugs, gangs, and other worldly vices. It's a live-in situation where these men are taught the Word of God every day for about four hours and then they work the rest of the day. They are supervised twenty-four hours a day, are taught things about self-discipline and responsibility, and a work ethic is developed in them. This ministry gets some marvelous, life-changing results with the men there because the Word of God is constantly taught while the love of God is shown to them.

There was a young man who had been at Canaan Land for about six weeks and had been given a weekend furlough to visit his family. This young man owned a little Toyota truck that was his pride and joy because it was the only thing he owned in this world. During that weekend furlough, the young man had run into a guy he used to be in the drug business with. This drug dealer told him, "You ripped me off on some drugs, so I'm taking your truck." He knew that the young man from Canaan Land had gone straight and wasn't about to go to the police because it would jeopardize his freedom.

When that young man returned to Canaan Land, he was totally dejected and downcast because he had lost his truck to that thug. The staff ministered to him that morning just before I got there and told him, "Look, God loves you. Why don't we just get in agreement that He will cause that truck to be returned to you?" They prayed and agreed together, and then later that morning I arrived and ministered to the men there.

When I had finished ministering, Mac Gober (the founder of Canaan Land) and another minister friend and I went out to eat. We were in my vehicle, and I was driving on the interstate to go to a local restaurant. As I took the exit off the interstate, I noticed a little black Toyota truck in front of us. It caught my eye because instead of "TOYOTA" on the tailgate, someone had painted over the first T and O and the last T and A. All that was left was "YO." Mac also noticed it and exclaimed, "That's our guy's truck! Follow him!" I immediately reacted and started following that little black truck.

Years ago, before I was in ministry, I was a deputy sheriff. I enjoyed that job, and I was good at it. Therefore, when I learned that the truck we were following was the one the young man had lost to this drug dealer, my old police training kicked in and I slipped into surveillance mode. The driver didn't know we were following him, and he led us into the worst part of town before he pulled over and parked. I went on past him, did a U-turn, and pulled right in front of him. This is an old police trick that makes it nearly impossible for someone to drive off. I have to admit I was enjoying this until I remembered that I wasn't a police officer anymore, and I wasn't armed.

Mac jumped out of the truck and walked up to the guy's window. Before the guy could do anything, Mac flipped out some kind of volunteer fireman or auxiliary police badge and then quickly shoved it back in his pocket and said, "Show me your registration papers for this truck."

The driver stammered a minute and then said, "Well, I don't have them with me."

Mac said, "We've been told this truck has been used in some illegal drug activity and, since you don't have any registration papers, we're going to impound it."

This whole thing happened pretty quickly, but by this time I could tell that the initial shock had worn off, and the drug dealer was starting to think about losing the truck. There was something about the look in his eyes that concerned me that this might not go down as we thought. We hadn't taken time to formulate a plan or consider what might happen. We just went after that truck because we were in the right, and this guy was wrong.

Because I had just come from ministering, I was dressed in a coat and tie, and so was the other minister with me. I figured this guy might think we were detectives. So I said to the other minister, "Get out of the car, watch me, and do what I do."

As I opened the door and got out of the car I made eye contact with the guy and reached inside my coat like I was armed and reaching for a weapon. The other minister did the same thing. The guy in the truck didn't know what was going on, but he decided not to take any chances and to just cooperate. He didn't know I was just reaching inside my coat to scratch my ribs! But he got all his stuff out of the truck, and we "impounded" it by taking the keys and driving off with it.

After getting something to eat, we drove back to Canaan Land and returned the young man's truck to him. You should have seen his reaction! He had just prayed that morning, and that afternoon his truck was back in his possession! God demonstrated His love and faithfulness to perform His Word.

What you should understand from this story is that we were bold to act because we knew we were right and represented the owner of that truck. We weren't trying to be tough guys or to assert ourselves for no reason. We knew the owner of the truck and that he had ownership rights to it. We knew that the one who currently possessed the truck did not. The thief had no ownership rights whatsoever. What was he going to do? Call the police? He stole the guy's truck by bullying and treachery! We were on solid legal ground as the owner's representatives.

When you understand your rights of ownership as a joint-heir with Jesus, and you know what is legally yours, it is not difficult to have aggressive faith to possess it. This kind of faith doesn't give up and say, "Oh well, I guess I missed it," if possession doesn't come right away. Bold, persevering faith says, "That's mine. I don't care what anybody says or what happens. God gave that to me and it's mine." When you know what belongs to you, the power of God will rise up in you to boldly step out and possess what is rightfully yours.

Ownership and Childlike Faith

In Luke 18:17 Jesus said, "Verily I say unto you, Whosoever shall not receive the Kingdom of God as a little child shall in no wise enter therein." How does a little child act about things that have been promised to them? They don't think twice about saying, "Give it to me. It's mine!" It reminds me of a child's T-shirt I saw that read, "If you've got it, it's mine." Little children just consider that they are entitled to enjoy everything their parents have, and Jesus said we were to have that same attitude toward our Heavenly Father.

Some Christians think more along the lines of God making them suffer by withholding what they need, whether it's money to pay their bills, wisdom to run a business, or good health to live the life He's called them to live. They need to learn what is legally theirs as joint-heirs with Jesus Christ. Then their faith would rise up to possess what God desires them to have.

I challenge you to meditate on your position in Jesus Christ. Consider the benefits and privileges of being a joint-heir with Him. Knowing your rights of ownership as a child of God will give your faith in Him a whole new dimension of confidence and joy as you meet the obstacles and trials of this life.

CHAPTER 6

Your Right to Be Whole

When you know God loves you, you know He wants you healthy and whole. By just reading His Word, you can know He wants you healed of any sickness or disease. First Peter 2:24 says, "by whose stripes ye were healed," and Isaiah 53:5 says, "But he was wounded for our transgressions, he was bruised for our iniquities: the chastisement of our peace was upon him; and with his stripes we are healed." Jesus paid for your healing with stripes.

Some biblical scholars will argue that "healing" means only spiritual healing, but that interpretation doesn't line up with God's character or the literal meanings of the Greek and Hebrew words translated "healed" in those verses of Scripture. The Hebrew word for "healed" in Isaiah 53:4 is *rapha*, which means "to mend...to cure...heal...make whole."[1] The Greek word for "healed" in 1 Peter 2:24 is *iaomai*, which means "to cure (literally or figuratively):—heal, make whole."[2]

When Jesus paid for our healing, He paid for all of it: spirit, soul, and body.

Jesus demonstrated God's will for us to be whole spiritually, physically, and emotionally in this life by healing people and delivering them from bondage while He was here on this earth. In fact, He never refused to heal anyone and always said it was His will to heal them. And in case you're thinking that it was only Jesus who wanted those people healed, the Gospel of John proves that God the Father, Jesus, and the Holy Spirit worked together and were in absolute agreement with everything Jesus did.

Jesus saith unto him, Have I been so long time with you, and yet hast thou not known me, Philip? he that hath seen me hath seen the Father; and how sayest thou then, Show us the Father?

Believest thou not that I am in the Father, and the Father in me? the words that I speak unto you I speak not of myself: but the Father that dwelleth in me, he doeth the works.

John 14:9-10

Then answered Jesus and said unto them, Verily, verily, I say unto you, The Son can do nothing of himself, but what he seeth the Father do: for what things soever he doeth, these also doeth the Son likewise.

John 5:19

I can of mine own self do nothing: as I hear, I judge: and my judgment is just; because I seek not mine own will, but the will of the Father which hath sent me.

John 5:30

Jesus didn't do anything that wasn't in total agreement with the Father. He and the Father are one. We can also say that He didn't do anything that was not in total agreement with the Holy Spirit, because the Holy Spirit always acts in accordance with the will of the Father and the Living Word, Jesus.

In Luke, chapter 13, we read the story of Jesus healing a woman who had been bent over for eighteen years. This account gives us some valuable and notable insight into God's will for healing as demonstrated and spoken by Jesus.

He [Jesus] was teaching in one of the synagogues on the sabbath. And, behold, there was a woman which had a spirit of infirmity eighteen years, and was bowed together, and could in no wise lift up herself.

Luke 13:10-11 [brackets mine]

A person can get really tired and discouraged after eighteen years of being bowed over, unable to stand upright. Jesus saw this woman as He was teaching, and He was so moved with compassion for her that He stopped His sermon to minister to her.

When Jesus saw her, he called her to him, and said unto her, Woman, thou art loosed from thine infirmity.

And he laid his hands on her: and immediately she was made straight, and glorified God.

And the ruler of the synagogue answered with indignation, because that Jesus had healed on the sabbath day, and said unto the people, There are six days in which men ought to work: in them therefore come and be healed, and not on the sabbath day.

The Lord then answered him, and said, Thou hypocrite, doth not each one of you on the sabbath loose his ox or his ass from the stall, and lead him away to watering?

And ought not this woman, being a daughter of Abraham, whom Satan hath bound, lo, these eighteen years, be loosed from this bond on the sabbath day?

Luke 13:12-16

I like the way Jesus answered the ruler of the synagogue. Jesus set some things straight. Notice that both the ruler and Jesus used the word "ought."

The Sabbath was the most holy day of the week, and the ruler said no one *ought* to be healed on the Sabbath. But this ruler had no idea what "holy" meant to God, so Jesus corrected him and said, "No, *this* is exactly how it *ought* to be," and He healed her. Being holy and being whole is the same thing to God. And because He's the same yesterday, today, and forever (Hebrews 13:8); if it *ought* to have been that way then, it *ought* to be that way now! Jesus wants to heal at all times and in all situations, including on the Sabbath.

Three Issues Settled

Now that we have established that all three members of the Godhead are in agreement, and the Word of God clearly states that you ought to be healed and whole, I want to point out three major issues that are settled in Luke's account of the woman Jesus healed on the Sabbath Day.

First, we see that Satan had caused this woman's affliction. Specifically, Luke 13:11 said that she was bound with a spirit of infirmity. And verse 16 states that her bondage was satanic in origin; it was not from God. God did not put this infirmity on her to make her humble or to teach her something. She was under attack from a demon of infirmity.

God does not make people sick! That truth is fundamental to receiving from Him. You've got to know that He is the author of blessing and goodness, and Satan is the one who binds people with all manner of destructive things. Sickness and disease come either directly from Satan or as a consequence of sin, which originated with him. Jesus took care of both when He died and was resurrected from the grave!

> *You, being dead in your sins and the uncircumcision of your flesh, hath he quickened together with him, having forgiven you all trespasses;*
> *Blotting out the handwriting of ordinances that was against us, which was contrary to us, and took it out of the way, nailing it to his cross;*

And having spoiled principalities and powers, he made a shew of them openly, triumphing over them in it.

Colossians 2:13-15

Jesus paid the debt for our sin, the origin and cause of all sickness and disease. He also defeated Satan and his army of demons, making "a shew of them openly." This means He paraded them like a conquering general of war, who would publicly humiliate the kings and military powers he had just completely defeated. The first issue that Jesus settled was that *sickness and disease come from the enemy and not from God.*

The second issue that Jesus settled was that this woman *ought* to be healed. When she was bent over, things were not as they ought to be. By healing the woman, Jesus demonstrated how things ought to be. Christians *ought* to be healed, standing straight and strong in Him. It is not God's will for us to be bound by the enemy, struggling just to survive, and unable to do or to be severely hindered in doing what He has called us to do. He wants us whole—spirit, soul, and body.

The third issue settled the ownership question, "Who does healing belong to?" Jesus said, "Ought not this woman, being a daughter of Abraham...." She had a covenant with God as a daughter of Abraham, and for that reason she ought to be healed! Romans 4:16 says that Abraham is the spiritual father of all believers. Therefore, all believers should be loosed from any bondage of the enemy. All believers *ought* to be healed!

When Jesus saw this woman, He called her to Him. Note the exact words He said to her: "Woman, thou art loosed." We don't talk that way today, but if Jesus were standing in front of you right now and you were bound by a spirit of infirmity, He would say, "Son or daughter of Abraham, child of God, you are loosed from this infirmity." He would not say, "I'm going to loose you" or "You are going to be loosed." That would put your healing somewhere in the future. Jesus would say, "You are loosed from this bondage and infirmity." Why? Because He would be speaking of your legal status as a child of God. With His stripes and His blood, Jesus has already purchased your healing!

That crippled woman had legal standing to be healed as a daughter of Abraham. Don't you know that when she heard Jesus' words, it came as news to her that she was loosed, that she was healed? I think this came as a shock, as a total revelation to her. She didn't know she was loosed, but what happened when the Word of God was spoken to her? Faith arose in her heart! Romans 10:17 says, "For then faith cometh by hearing and hearing by the Word of God."

This woman may have been in shock to hear that she was loosed from her infirmity, but these words were the Word of God and they ignited faith in her heart. She didn't just hear an offhanded comment from someone teaching in the synagogue. She heard the Word of God spoken by the Anointed One, that she had a legal right to be whole. And that news brought revelation to her, causing her to rise up and possess what was already hers as a daughter of Abraham. When Jesus put His hands on her, she was immediately made straight and began to glorify God.

The Seed of Abraham

When Jesus asked, "Ought not this woman, being a daughter of Abraham, be loosed from this bondage on the Sabbath day?" He was showing her legal status for healing because she was tied to Abraham. It defined her as being part of a covenant. Jesus made a legal statement, a covenant statement, because Abraham's relationship with God was a legal covenant. A covenant is a contract, a legal agreement.

Covenant is a word frequently used today in reference to construction, building houses and neighborhoods. For example, when you buy a house in a subdivision, you may have to agree to certain *covenants* that govern what kind of house you will build and how you will take care of your property.

I have some friends who bought a house on a lake, and one of the neighborhood covenants was that they agreed not to put a speedboat on the lake. They could use a little boat with a trolling motor, but they could not operate a powerboat on the lake. Another type of covenant you might encounter would limit the ways you would landscape your yard or decorate the outside of your house. These covenants are legally binding, and when you agree to them, it gives the neighborhood association the authority to enforce them.

When Jesus brought Abraham into the picture, He was saying that this woman had legal rights. By linking her to Abraham, He told her and all mankind that healing has been available to believers since God's covenant with Abraham. The children of Abraham, all those who have faith in God as Abraham had faith in Him, receive all the blessings of Abraham.

This woman was a daughter of Abraham, but she didn't know the rights of her covenant. She didn't know she was loosed. She didn't know she was free. She didn't know this spirit of infirmity could not hold her unless she allowed it to hold her. When Jesus placed His hands on her, she became the proud possessor of the deliverance that was hers legally. She was healed because she had a covenant as a daughter of Abraham.

Furthermore, if this woman was heir to healing as the seed of Abraham, then so are you!

If you be Christ's, then are you Abraham's seed and heirs according to the promise.

Galatians 3:29

Who was Abraham's seed? Jesus! Jesus is also the seed of the woman whom God said would crush the head of the snake. (Genesis 3:15.) Old Testament saints were saved because they put their faith in the Promised Seed. New Testament saints are saved because they put their faith in the Seed who has come,

Jesus Christ. You are heir to healing because you put your faith in Him, you were born again, and now you live in Him. You are actually in the Seed, and the Seed is in you!

Pleasing God

I think back to so many times when I sat in services, heard the Word of God, and faith rose up in my heart. Lights went on, and I thought, *Wow! I see who I am in Him. I see what I have in Him.* That was exactly what the woman in the synagogue experienced when Jesus told her she had a covenant that included her physical healing. Her legal rights guaranteed that she should not be bowed over, and when she saw that, she became whole the moment Jesus touched her.

Ownership is important to understand because when you know you own something, it changes the way you look at it. On the subject of healing, if you are sick and somebody says God *will* heal you, your healing becomes something He has to do for you in the future. Then you begin thinking about what you need to do to earn that healing, what you need to do to qualify for healing. But when you understand that in Jesus Christ you have a legal right to be whole, that in Him you already are healed, you operate in faith instead of relying on your own works to possess your healing.

Once it is settled in your heart that you are healed in Jesus Christ, then you can release your faith in Him and His Word to physically possess what He's already given you. Healing belongs to you. The blessings of God belong to you.

It doesn't please God for someone to say, "Oh, I wouldn't want to be presumptuous. I wouldn't want to be greedy about the blessings of God." When they do that, they're showing no respect or gratitude for what Jesus paid dearly to give them. Furthermore, they're not partaking of God's divine nature by pursuing His promises to them, and this does not please Him! That's why Hebrews 11:6 is so important to remember at all times.

> *Without faith it is impossible to please him: for he that cometh to God must believe that he is, and that he is a rewarder of them that diligently seek him.*
>
> Hebrews 11:6

God is not pleased if you do not use the faith He has given you to possess the blessings He's provided for you. We've now come full circle back to what we talked about in the first chapters of this book. Everything in the Christian life hangs on our daily, personal intimacy with God. We're not just trying to load up on blessings for ourselves. We don't want to be healed just so we can go to the casino, get drunk, and lose all the money He's given us to steward. God made us whole in Christ Jesus so that we could walk with Him, become like Him, and do what He's called us to do.

For eighteen years that woman was bent over at the waist, probably in pain. How could she get married, have children, and run a household? How could she go to the marketplace and buy and sell? How could she even gather firewood for the fire and cook the meals? Whatever she was destined to accomplish as a daughter of Abraham was severely hampered because of her infirmity, and that did not please God! Satan and that spirit of infirmity were pleased, however. They were smiling for eighteen years because God's daughter was bound and crippled, unable to accomplish His will for her life. The devil might even have convinced her that God had cursed her, brought this infirmity on her, and then forgot her. But Jesus changed all that! When He told her who she was and what was hers as "Abraham's seed," she saw that God hadn't cursed her and forgotten her. He had blessed her and always loved her. She just didn't know it!

You are also Abraham's seed and heir of the promise. Even better, you are in Jesus Christ and He is in you. His Spirit dwells in your spirit and you are one with the Father, the Son, and the Holy Spirit. His Word is living and powerful in your heart, and the measure of faith He gave you to be saved can now be used to possess everything else that He has provided. Like the woman who was loosed of the spirit of infirmity, you also are loosed to glorify God in every area of your life.

CHAPTER 7

Possessing Your Inheritance

In Luke 13:10-16, Jesus loosed the woman, who had been held in bondage for eighteen years by a spirit of infirmity. Healing didn't come into existence at that moment. Healing had been hers as long as she was a daughter of Abraham. However, although she had *ownership* of all the blessings of God, she didn't *possess* her healing because she didn't know her covenant rights.

When you study the subject of faith, you must understand that there is a difference between ownership and possession. This is what Jesus illustrated through the woman in the synagogue. Ownership is a legal standing and is determined by who paid for what is owned. Possession, on the other hand, is a practical, experiential matter, not a legal issue. You can own something legally and never possess it experientially.

When my children were growing up, I agreed that if they would work and save their money, when they wanted to get a car I would put in half the price. The title was in my name and I said, "As long as you go by the rules, buy the gas, and pay for the insurance, you can drive the car." Then, when the time came for them to leave home and be on their own, I signed the car over to them. In all those years, even though I legally owned those cars, they were rarely ever in my possession. I had ownership rights but did not possess what I owned.

You can also possess a thing without owning it, as my kids did with the cars we bought that were in my name. They possessed the cars but did not own them. But as believers we not only legally *own* our inheritance in Christ Jesus, we also can *possess* it by faith. What the devil tries to do is to keep us from possessing it, or if we do possess it, he will try to steal it from us. Thank God, Jesus gave us authority over the enemy! (See Luke 10:19.)

If you purchased a vehicle, paid for it in full, and had the title free and clear, you would own that vehicle. If someone stole it, they would possess it; but they would not own it. You would be looking for the one who took it, calling the police and demanding that vehicle be returned to you because you are the legal owner. Legal rights of ownership will ignite your faith to possess what is yours.

Faith: Your Title Deed

Jesus paid for our salvation and "all things that pertain unto life and godliness" (2 Peter 1:3) when He was crucified and resurrected. As born-again believers in Him and joint-heirs with Him, we now *own* "all spiritual blessings in Christ Jesus" (Ephesians 1:3). They are ours legally, but we must *possess* them by faith. Our faith in God and His Word is what causes us to actually possess what is ours in Christ Jesus.

*Faith is the assurance (the confirmation, the title deed) of the things [we] hope for, being the proof of things [we] do not see **and** the conviction of their reality [faith perceiving as real fact what is not revealed to the senses].*

Hebrews 11:1 AMP

We read here that faith is "the title deed" to the things we hope for but do not see. I like that translation especially because it calls our faith "the title deed," and a title deed is a legal document. This wording points to the fact that we have legal rights and privileges in Jesus Christ.

He that cometh to God must believe that he is, and that he is a rewarder of them that diligently seek him.

Hebrews 11:6

Legally, when we come to God believing in Him and seeking Him diligently in all matters of our lives, we are rewarded. There are rewards when we operate according to the covenant we have with Him. In God's dealings with mankind, everything is done on the basis of covenant. He is always just and right, which means He does everything legally and according to the covenant or agreement He has made.

Covenant, then, is the legal side of our inheritance; while faith is the method by which we possess in the natural realm what God has already provided in the spirit realm. When we received Jesus as our Lord and Savior, we became legal owners of His benefits. While ownership is ours, possessing all that we have been given can be accomplished only by faith.

The Bible tells us there are two parts to possessing what is legally ours.

1. Believe in your heart.

2. Confess with your mouth what you believe in your heart.

If thou shalt confess with thy mouth the Lord Jesus, and shalt believe in thine heart that God hath raised him from the dead, thou shalt be saved.
For with the heart man believeth unto righteousness; and with the mouth confession is made unto salvation.

Romans 10:9-10

Verily I say unto you, That whosoever shall say unto this mountain, Be thou removed, and be thou cast into the sea; and shall not doubt in his heart, but shall believe that those things which he saith shall come to pass; he shall have whatsoever he saith.
Therefore I say unto you, What things soever ye desire, when ye pray, believe that ye receive them, and ye shall have them.

Mark 11:23-24

You received salvation by believing in your heart and confessing with your mouth, and that is the same way you possess everything that is legally yours in Christ Jesus. You say what you believe. How do you come to believe something?

Faith cometh by hearing, and hearing by the word of God.

Romans 10:17

Before you were born again you heard the Word regarding salvation, faith arose in your heart, and you received Jesus as your Lord and Savior. Now that you are saved you hear God's Word regarding healing, financial prosperity, divine protection, and other issues of life. Again, God's Word causes faith to rise in your heart because He tells you what is legally yours, what belongs to you as His child. Scripture declares and establishes your rights of ownership, and when you know you own it you can have faith to possess it. The first part of possessing what belongs to you is believing in your heart that it is yours. You must see it with your spiritual eyes.

How do you see something with your spiritual eyes? You simply choose to come into agreement with what God says and to see things as God sees them. If He sees you healed by the stripes of Jesus, then you must decide to believe in your heart that you are healed and to see yourself that way. Remind yourself who you are and what you have in Jesus Christ by meditating and speaking the Word until you know it's yours and see yourself possessing it. Remember, faith is the substance of things hoped for and the title deed of things not seen with the natural eye. But you can see things with the eye of faith by choosing to see things as God sees them.

Make the decision that God's Word settles it for you no matter what circumstances or people tell you. Walking in faith means you see what is legally yours, you rest in the knowledge that God is faithful and His Word stands forever, and then you never quit. Through faith and patience you inherit the promises of God (Hebrews 6:12), and you can always know that it is only a matter of time before what you have seen in your spirit will be fully manifested.

Believing and Confessing Work Together

Believing and confessing what we believe work together in our walk of faith. Once we make the decision to agree with God's Word, sometimes it takes awhile of confessing and declaring what we believe before it settles in our hearts and we "know that we know that we know" that we have what we say.

I ministered to a man once who wanted to be free from an addiction but he just couldn't seem to get a handle on it. No method worked for him. I suggested that every time he had a need for a fix or was being driven by his flesh for that nasty habit he should confess, "Thank God, I am free. I am delivered and have no need or desire for anything that is not pleasing to God." He started doing that, and after a season he realized that he no longer had those urges and drives working in him. One day the truth hit him that he was free. The Word had worked a miracle in him!

> *Verily I say unto you, That whosoever shall say unto this mountain,*
> *Be thou removed, and be thou cast into the sea; and shall not doubt*
> *in his heart, but shall believe that those things which he saith shall*
> *come to pass; he shall have whatsoever he saith.*
>
> Mark 11:23

This man knew that legally the blood of Jesus had set him free from every destructive addiction in his life. When he confessed that truth over and over, faith came by hearing and he began to believe it and see himself free in his heart. Finally, as he confessed that exceeding great and precious promise, he partook of God's divine nature to the point where even his natural mind and body didn't cooperate with those fleshly desires anymore. (2 Peter 1:4.) It was settled in his heart and became reality in his life.

Do you see how God has set up this walk of faith so that as we stand on His Word and believe Him for what we need in life, we become more like Him? Confessing Scripture to receive what is ours and what God has provided for this life changes how we think, speak, act, and even look. By using our faith and possessing what God has given us, we are being transformed into the image of Jesus! That is how powerful our faith is, and that is why the enemy will do anything he can to stop us from trusting God and His Word for everything in life.

If the enemy or anyone else challenges us about what is ours or tries to take it from us, we simply point to what the Bible says. We believe and confess the Word to press through and defeat the devil at every turn. When he tries to make us sick, tempt us to sin, or steal our joy, all we have to do is what Jesus did. We simply say, "It is written," and quote what God has said about the matter. You can do it like this:

Say, "Sickness, spirit of infirmity, you must leave my body now because it is written in 1 Peter 2:24 and Mark 16:17 that I am healed by the stripes of Jesus and I have authority over all demons. Thank You, Jesus, that I am whole today."

Say, "Satan, it is written in 2 Corinthians 5:21 that Jesus was made to be sin so that I could be made righteous in Him. I praise God that I overcome every temptation to sin because I now have His strength to say no to it."

Say, "Depression and discouragement, it is written in Nehemiah 8:10 and 2 Corinthians 12:9 that the joy of the Lord is my strength and His strength is made perfect in my weakness. I thank God that I am free from depression and discouragement."

If you don't know what is written about you or your situation, then it is time to find out!

Study to shew thyself approved unto God, a workman that needeth not to be ashamed, rightly dividing the word of truth.

2 Timothy 2:15

It's always a shame for children of God to be afflicted and beaten down when Jesus died to provide us with abundant life. In this verse Timothy is exhorting us to study God's Word, find out what is ours, and use our faith to possess it. Faith pleases God, because when we exercise our faith in Him, we begin to think like He thinks and speak like He speaks, calling those things that be not as though they were (Romans 4:17). In other words, God sees it in the spirit and calls it forth in the natural, and we are to imitate Him and act the same way.

We should all aspire to be mature sons and daughters of God who have studied to show ourselves approved, rightly dividing the Word and calling things that be not as though they were. Talking like God is not just something we do whenever we get in a predicament and need a miracle. Talking like God is part of living the abundant life of faith, which is ours as new creatures in Christ Jesus.

Confession: The Word of Your Testimony

I love to quote and meditate on the Word of God to get it down in my heart. I do it all the time. Then, if a situation or crisis comes, the Word is there inside me, ready to come forth as a two-edged sword and work in my behalf. One such verse is found in Revelation 12:11, "They overcame him by the blood of the Lamb, and by the word of their testimony." When I face a tough situation, this Word will come to me and I know there is nothing I cannot overcome because of His blood and my testimony of His goodness toward me.

One day the Holy Spirit rose up inside me and confronted me concerning how I was applying this Scripture. He said, "You're not operating in the fullness of what that verse means when it speaks of overcoming by the word of your testimony. Your testimony is not just repeating a Scripture over and over until you have memorized it so you can quote it verbatim. This verse speaks of your testimony as your consistent confession as you live your life."

Your testimony encompasses your entire manner of life, not just what you say when the pressure is on. If you hold fast to your confession of God's Word and it becomes the way you live your life, the way you think, the way you act and react, then you *will* overcome. The blood is the legal side; Jesus shed His blood to pay the debt for your sin and provide redemption. Your testimony is the practical side; you come into agreement with the Word of God, what Jesus provided for you, what He gave you to possess, and live it daily.

When we hear the word "testimony," most of us picture somebody standing up and telling how they got saved. There's a truth to that, but it goes beyond how we got saved into how we got healed, became prosperous, were made righteous and overcame sin, discovered joy, and experienced the peace that passes understanding. Our testimony is how we gained all these things through Jesus Christ, and they became a part of our everyday experience.

Years ago Brother Kenneth E. Hagin and his wife were in Birmingham for a ministers' conference. While he was here, he and I and our wives went to lunch and then to a local mall with a huge open atrium and a high glass ceiling. While the ladies shopped, Brother Hagin and I sat on a bench and talked. I loved listening to him and always looked forward to being with him so I could draw from his years of ministry and wisdom.

On this particular occasion I said, "Brother Hagin, it's amazing to me the difference in your ministry and so many other ministers. There's such a maturity about your ministry, while others, even though they're good and solid and Word of Faith oriented, just lack that maturity. When I'm in your services, listening to your tapes, or even reading your books, there's a difference. Others may use the same Scriptures and illustrations, but it's different when you teach it. Why is that?"

Brother Hagin leaned back and looked around. Then he said, "Well, I'll tell you. We're sitting here in this mall. This place is big enough that if I were to yell out a word or a name, you'd hear an echo coming back. Now that echo would be saying the same thing that my voice said, but there would be a difference between the voice and the echo."

I thought that was pretty profound and I said, "Yeah, I can see that."

He went on to say, "You see, here's the difference. I'm not teaching somebody else's theory. I'm not teaching what I heard somebody else teach or what I read in someone else's book. The things I teach are the things that I've lived, and some I've lived almost all my life and have proved out. So many of these other people are teaching the right message, but they haven't lived it and proven it out in their lives. So that's what makes me a voice and some of these other folks are just an echo."

I thought, *Lord, that's great! That explains it!* And then I thought, *Now wait a minute. Brother Hagin was healed of an incurable heart disease as a young man, and he's walked through some things I haven't walked through.* So I asked him, "What about the rest of us? You were healed at sixteen years old. I didn't go through that. What's happened to you hasn't happened to me. Is there any hope for the rest of us?"

He said, "Oh, sure there is! If you'll just stay with it and be faithful, then God will make you a voice."

That day Brother Hagin gave me insight and understanding about some things of the Spirit. He had caught the spirit of faith by revelation from God's Word and applied it first to his own life. As a dying boy he read in his grandmother's Methodist Bible that by the stripes of Jesus he was healed. He believed what the Word said, got up off his bed of affliction, and began to act healed. As he acted on the Word of God, he gained strength and was made whole. Then he began to tell people how the Word of God had healed him. Throughout his life he continued to walk in and minister to others the revelation the Holy Spirit had given him from God's Word. He lived and ministered in that way for over sixty years, and all these things were the word of his testimony. He stayed faithful to the Word of God until the end of his walk here on this earth.

Your testimony consists of how you live and not just what you say or know. Your confession is more than just saying the Word over and over. When you believe it and live it, you prove the Word of God in the challenges of your daily life. You become a strong voice of faith and not just another echo because you have overcome by the blood of the Lamb and the word of your testimony. In this way, you possess all God has given you in Christ Jesus.

The process of possessing your inheritance is the walk of faith. You choose to have faith in God and His Word rather than having faith in your circumstances, the opinions of people, or the lies of the enemy. You bring your thoughts and speech into agreement with God's Word. Then the inheritance Jesus died to give you will manifest in your life, and you will become a powerful voice to those around you.

CHAPTER 8

Talking in God's Ear

The words we speak are vital to possessing our inheritance. What we say or don't say does not affect our ownership rights, but it will affect what we possess. What we say will determine what we have, no matter where we are or who we are talking to (Mark 11:23).

Numbers, chapter 13, tells the story of the twelve spies who went into the land of Canaan. In verse 2 God instructed Moses to send these men to search the land, *which I give unto the children of Israel.* After searching out the land, two of the spies, Joshua and Caleb, brought back a good report, saying, "Let us go up at once, and possess it; for we are well able to overcome it" (Numbers 13:30). The other ten spies came back and reported that there were giants in the land who were too big to conquer. These ten men chose to be afraid instead of having faith in what God said, that He had given them the land. The Bible calls this an *evil* report!

They brought up an evil report of the land which they had searched unto the children of Israel, saying, The land, through which we have gone to search it, is a land that eateth up the inhabitants thereof; and all the people that we saw in it are men of a great stature.

And there we saw the giants, the sons of Anak, which come of the giants: and we were in our own sight as grasshoppers, and so we were in their sight.

Numbers 13:32-33

It is evil to disagree with God's Word, and especially to argue that you cannot possess what He says He has given you. It is evil to regard anything of this world as bigger than God or His Word!

We need to be like Joshua and Caleb, who brought back a good report. They chose to have faith in what God had told them in Numbers 13:2, "Search the land of Canaan, which I *give* unto the children of Israel." Because they had faith in God's Word, Joshua and Caleb did possess the land later, but the other spies and the rest of the people did not. They did not possess the land because of their words.

All the congregation lifted up their voice, and cried; and the people wept that night.

And all the children of Israel murmured against Moses and against Aaron: and the whole congregation said unto them, Would God that we had died in the land of Egypt! or would God we had died in this wilderness!

Numbers 14:1-2

These people were murmuring to each other and complaining publicly. This was a public discussion, and all the children of Israel, with the exception of Moses, Joshua, and Caleb, said they could not take the land and wished they had died in Egypt or in the wilderness. Now look at God's response.

> The LORD spake unto Moses and unto Aaron, saying,
> How long shall I bear with this evil congregation, which murmur against me? I have heard the murmurings of the children of Israel, which they murmur against me.
> Say unto them, As truly as I live, saith the LORD, as ye have spoken in mine ears, so will I do to you.
>
> Numbers 14:26-28

These people were not praying or confessing the Word in church or in their prayer closets. They were talking in public, debating the issue, and taking a vote. They didn't think about who might be listening. They didn't think God was taking notes on everything they said, but He did. He said, "What you said in public, *you said in my ears. And what you said in my ears is what you're going to get.*"

> Your carcases shall fall in this wilderness; and all that were numbered of you, according to your whole number, from twenty years old and upward, which have murmured against me.
> Doubtless ye shall not come into the land, concerning which I sware to make you dwell therein, save Caleb the son of Jephunneh, and Joshua the son of Nun.
> But your little ones, which ye said should be a prey, them will I bring in, and they shall know the land which ye have despised.

But as for you, your carcases, they shall fall in this wilderness.

Numbers 14:29-32

The lesson we learn from this is to ALWAYS speak in faith! We must always speak in agreement with God's Word. Jesus is our example, and He always spoke in agreement with Scripture. In fact, He said, "Lo, I come (in the volume of the book it is written of me,) to do thy will, O God" (Hebrews 10:7). His entire life as a human being was lived in accordance with the written Word of God.

Jesus Heard Thomas

Jesus also hears everything we say. After His resurrection, all the disciples were gathered together except Thomas, and Jesus appeared to them. This should not have been a surprise to them; Jesus had told His disciples that He was going to die and rise again. He said, "Destroy this temple, and in three days I will raise it up" (John 2:19). Then, in John 10:17-19, Jesus said, "I lay down my life, that I might take it again. No man taketh it from me, but I lay it down of myself. I have power to lay it down, and I have power to take it again."

They had all been told what was coming, but none of them could grasp it or believe it until after the resurrection, when Jesus appeared to everyone but Thomas. On the evening of the resurrection Jesus appeared to the disciples, who were locked in a room, hiding for fear of the Jews (John 20:19). He breathed on them, saying, "Receive ye the Holy Ghost" (v. 22). Only then did they understand fully that Jesus was alive.

After Jesus left them that night, Thomas showed up and the disciples told him what had happened. Notice what Thomas said to them.

> *The other disciples therefore said unto him, We have seen the Lord. But he said unto them, Except I shall see in his hands the print of the nails, and put my finger into the print of the nails, and thrust my hand into his side, I will not believe.*
>
> John 20:25

When Thomas heard that Jesus had appeared to the other disciples, he said, *Unless I see it for myself and touch Him I will not believe.*

Eight days later Jesus appeared to His disciples again, and this time Thomas was with them.

> *After eight days again his disciples were within, and Thomas with them: then came Jesus, the doors being shut, and stood in the midst, and said, Peace be unto you.*
> *Then saith he to Thomas, Reach hither thy finger, and behold my hands; and reach hither thy hand, and thrust it into my side: and be not faithless, but believing.*
> *And Thomas answered and said unto him, My LORD and my God.*
>
> John 20:26-28

I call to your attention the fact that Jesus had heard what Thomas had said eight days earlier. That's why He told Thomas not to be faithless but to believe. Thomas had just been hanging out with the other disciples, talking with his friends. Jesus was not physically present, but He heard every word of doubt and unbelief Thomas spoke.

God is always listening! He hears not only our prayers, but He also listens to every word we say. No matter where we are or who we are with, everything we say is like talking in His ears. This is why it is so important for us to speak in agreement with Him and His Word or to keep silent until we can. We cannot walk in faith and speak in opposition to what God has written in the Bible.

Nothing Is Hid From Him

The great news is that God doesn't just hear *our* words. He also hears our *enemies'* words! You might remember this story of the Prophet Elisha and the king of Syria found in 2 Kings, chapter 6.

> *Then the king of Syria warred against Israel, and took counsel with his servants, saying, In such and such a place shall be my camp. And the man of God sent unto the king of Israel, saying, Beware that thou pass not such a place; for thither the Syrians are come down. And the king of Israel sent to the place which the man of God told him and warned him of, and saved himself there, not once nor twice.*

Therefore the heart of the king of Syria was sore troubled for this thing; and he called his servants, and said unto them, Will ye not shew me which of us is for the king of Israel?

And one of his servants said, None, my lord, O king: but Elisha, the prophet that is in Israel, telleth the king of Israel the words that thou speakest in thy bedchamber.

2 Kings 6:8-12

The king of Syria thought there was a spy among them who was reporting to the king of Israel. But he soon leaned from his servant that the prophet of God was the one who was telling their secrets.

How did Elisha know what the king had said in his bedchamber? How does a prophet get his information? From God! In order for God to tell Elisha what the king was planning, He had to have heard what the king had said in his bedchamber.

This is great news for us because God can tell us what the enemy is planning against us. Then we can use our faith and His Word to stop or defeat any attack that comes against us.

Remember: what you say in public, God hears. What you say to your friends, God hears. What you say even in the privacy of your bedchamber, God hears. And what you confess, you possess; therefore, be careful what you confess!

Covenant Talk and Covenant Walk

Whenever the Lord reveals a really powerful truth from His Word, the enemy will come in to bring extremism and perversion of that truth so that believers will reject it. There are extremes in many Bible doctrines that the devil has used to bring confusion and misconception, and he has effectively used these tactics to rob the body of Christ of life-changing revelation from the Word of God. The truth concerning the life of faith is no exception. It makes sense that the enemy would do anything he could to cause believers to shun any solid teaching of faith because faith is the key to pleasing God and receiving everything He has for His children.

Through the years there have been some believers who have misapplied, abused, and misunderstood the subject of faith. There have been other believers who really got an understanding of faith but they just didn't stick with it long enough to see the harvest of their labor. They didn't press in to get a solid understanding of their covenant ownership rights from God's Word and how to possess what was theirs.

Like every believer, I had to persevere and patiently stand on God's promises to possess what God had given me in the New Covenant. I had to ask myself, "Who owns my healing? I do. Why? Because Jesus paid for it and then He gave it to me. Who owns my right to prosper, my power to get wealth? I do.

Why? Because Jesus paid for it with His blood and He gave it to me."

Jesus said to me in His Word, "You and I are in covenant with one another. You and I are one. What's mine is yours and what's yours is mine."

Then I began to confess, "I'm in Him and He's in me. What's His is mine and what's mine is His. We are in covenant and we are one."

Covenant is very simple to understand, but to many Christians our covenant with God seems almost too good to be true. When they read about what is legally theirs in the Bible or hear solid teaching on their covenant rights, they still walk around in a cloud of uncertainty. They feel presumptuous and uncomfortable confessing what is rightfully theirs or even thinking in those terms. Consequently, they live from day to day thinking that whatever happens, whatever they gain or lose, is just God's will. They have never come to terms with their ownership rights or the responsibility God gives them to possess their inheritance by faith.

If God didn't want us to have this inheritance, why did He say in His Word that He gave it to us? Furthermore, it's not like He needs it! He didn't provide this great salvation and all it encompasses for Himself. He bought it for us because we are the ones who need it!

God has everything He needs, but He doesn't have everything He *wants*. He still wants to see His children prospering in every area of their lives. He wants to see His Kingdom come and His will done on earth as it is in Heaven. But He will never get what He wants if we refuse to believe what He has given us and then refuse to possess it! Believers are the only ones through whom He can bring Heaven to earth.

If believers adopt an attitude of false humility and remain sick, poor, and miserable, that is not Heaven on earth! Nor is it God's will. That is why it is false humility. That attitude denies who we are in Christ Jesus and ignores His provision.

True humility is acting on the truth that we are in Him and He is in us. We are partakers of the New Covenant in Jesus' blood; what is His is ours and what is ours is His. Paul said in Galatians 2:20, "I am crucified with Christ: nevertheless I live; yet not I, but Christ liveth in me: and the life which I now live in the flesh I live by the faith of the Son of God, who loved me, and gave himself for me."

Paul didn't just *talk* about covenant; he *lived* it. When he was stoned and left for dead, he defied death and rose up healed. When he was imprisoned, he praised God and was miraculously released. When he stood before kings and magistrates, he preached and taught about this great salvation that Jesus had died to give him. Paul never thought it arrogant or presumptuous to boldly confess his right standing with God because he knew God wanted him to have everything salvation entailed.

There is no lack of health, wisdom, peace, and prosperity in Heaven, and we are citizens of Heaven. As ambassadors of Christ in this earth, there should be no lack of these things where we are either. But if we don't believe we are owners of "all things that pertain unto life and godliness" (2 Peter 1:3), we will never possess them. Only when we know something is ours, that God gave it to us for our personal enjoyment, health, and well-being, can we step out in faith and partake of all He has provided.

Christians who fail to confess God's Word and fail to possess their inheritance by using the faith God has given them fall into the same category as the ten spies and the children of Israel who believed the evil report instead of the Word of God. God gave them the land, and instead of possessing it, they compared themselves to the giants. Instead of trusting God and taking Him at His Word, they acknowledged the giants and ignored God's promise to them. Believers who scoff at confessing and possessing their inheritance are either ignorant of what the Bible says or they have chosen to see themselves as unworthy sinners, refusing to acknowledge their position of righteous children of the Most High God.

There is no arrogance in seeing yourself the way God sees you and declaring it out loud. After all, He is the One who says you are the righteousness of God in Christ Jesus (2 Corinthians 5:21). That simple truth should make you more humble than ever! There is also no arrogance in acknowledging His great gift of salvation and all that includes. Again, if you really under-stand what He's given you in Jesus Christ, you can't help but be humble about it. You did nothing to earn it or deserve it, and therefore you can't take any credit for it.

Begin to speak the truth about yourself at all times because God is listening. You are always talking in His ears! Remember that He delights in hearing you proclaim that you see yourself the way He sees you. It gives Him pleasure to hear you grate-fully receive all He has freely and lovingly given to you through Jesus Christ, His Son. And nothing should hold you back from pleasing your Heavenly Father!

CHAPTER 9

A Different Way of Talking

Throughout the Bible, God's promises are usually declared in the past tense or the present tense. For example, in the case of healing in Isaiah 53:5, we read, "with his stripes we *are* healed." This is present tense because the Holy Spirit was showing Isaiah what was going to happen in the future. In the spirit Isaiah was walking with the Messiah, watching Him being beaten and crucified. Therefore, Isaiah wrote, "with his stripes we *are* healed," because that is what the Holy Spirit was showing him.

Later, in 1 Peter 2:24, the Holy Spirit reminded Peter of when Jesus was beaten and crucified and led him to write, "By whose stripes ye *were* healed." Peter saw it as an accomplished fact and wrote about it that way. Both Old Testament saints and New Testament saints are healed by the stripes of Jesus.

God tells us in 1 Corinthians 2:16 that we have the mind of Christ, which means we *already* have it. He says that He hasn't given us the spirit of fear but of power, love, and a sound mind (2 Timothy 1:7). God always speaks to us in the present tense or past tense, and the promises Jesus fulfilled in the New Testament are written in the past tense. Second Peter 1:3 tells us that He has already given us all things that pertain to life and godliness. He has already given us everything we need in this life and forever!

That is not the way most Christians talk. They don't think in terms of the provision of God being past tense, something already accomplished. Because they don't think that way, they don't talk like they are already healed or delivered.

Most believers say things like, "Well, I hope that I will get healed." It seems awkward and presumptuous to say, "I'm healed," when their body is wracked with pain. It sounds crazy to rejoice if they lose their job, saying, "I have everything I need in Jesus, and I'm not worried. I'm excited! He has another job waiting for me, a better job with better pay."

Who in the world talks like that? A peculiar people. A holy nation. Believers who understand what they own as joint-heirs with Jesus Christ and are determined to possess what He paid a dear price to give them. These are the ones who talk like they already have it. Yes, when you start talking like this it feels awkward, even embarrassing for a while. That is because every demon in hell is trying to get you to stop! They know that you are beginning to speak your way out of their evil influence and bondage to possess the blessings God has given you.

This way of thinking and speaking is radical and foreign to the world's way of thinking and speaking. The world's way says you can only possess that which is tangible, what you can see, hear, touch, smell, or taste. If your senses can't contact it, then it doesn't exist and it isn't real. But as spiritual children of God we walk by faith and not by sight. What we think and speak is not dependent on whether or not we can see it or touch it.

I sometimes illustrate this in meetings by simply calling on someone and asking them if they have a car. Once I called on a man who said he had a truck. I asked him, "Where is it? I don't see it. Does anyone here see this man's truck? He says he has one."

Then I looked at the man and said, "No one here has any physical evidence that you have a truck. How can you say that you have it?"

Whoever I have called on will always say, "Because I own it. I have a bill of sale, or a title."

The Word of God is our proof of ownership, and we possess what we own by believing in our heart that what God told us is true, then speaking with our mouths in agreement with what He told us. The man I called on could see his truck in his inner man. He could describe it to us. He knew what it felt like to drive it. And that's the way we need to talk about what is already ours in Christ Jesus, so that we can possess it in the natural as well.

When Jesus bore those stripes, hung on the Cross, shed His blood, and took our sin into hell, He paid the full price. He bought our complete salvation—spirit, soul, and body. Knowing the price He paid and that He died to provide everything we need should cause us to examine what is coming out of our mouths. Should we be saying, "I'm so sick. Why did God allow this to happen"? Shouldn't we say instead, "These aches and pains have to go because Jesus purchased my healing. By His stripes I am healed. Thank You, Lord, that I am whole in spirit, soul, and body!" When I know what is mine, I can boldly say that I have it. And when I confess it, I possess it!

Don't Complain—Talk to God

Your words have been stout against me, saith the LORD. Yet ye say, What have we spoken so much against thee?
Ye have said, It is vain to serve God: and what profit is it that we have kept his ordinance, and that we have walked mournfully before the LORD of hosts?

Malachi 3:13-14

Years ago, as I read this passage, I said to the Lord, "In all my years of pastoring (which had been about seventeen years at that time), I can't remember anyone saying that they thought it was vain to serve God." I said this because no matter what century or culture you live in, people have the same needs, desires, sins, flesh, and the devil to contend with. People today are no different from people in Malachi's time, so why hadn't I ever heard anyone say this?

Then, like I had a tape player in my heart, the Lord began to play back things that I had heard people say.

"Well Pastor, it's not working."

"It's too late."

"I don't have enough."

"I guess we'll just have to do without."

I realized that all those comments were really saying, "It is vain to serve God." Regardless of what we say or who we say it to, we know God hears what we say.

> Then they that feared the LORD spake often one to another: and the LORD hearkened, and heard it, and a book of remembrance was written before him for them that feared the LORD, and that thought upon his name.
> And they shall be mine, saith the LORD of hosts, in that day when I make up my jewels; and I will spare them, as a man spareth his own son that serveth him.
>
> Malachi 3:16-17

About those who spoke in faith and continued to trust Him, God said, "Those are my jewels. I'll deliver them like a man delivers his son who serves him." He heard what they were saying to each other and wrote it down! But what about the times you just need to speak your heart and work through your frustrations and fears? You may have times of testing when you just need help.

In order to get to a place of faith, sometimes we need to work through some things, to be honest about what we are thinking and feeling about our situation. As I study the Word of God, it is clear that the Lord is a lot more tolerant when you challenge *Him* about the way things are than when you complain to *others*. There were several times that Abraham and Moses, to name just two, went to the Lord and talked to Him about their situations.

In Genesis 18:20-33 Abraham was upset that God was going to destroy Sodom and Gomorrah. Instead of complaining to Sarah, he went straight to God and said, "God, You are not going to destroy those cities if there are righteous people there, are You?" In the end God did destroy the cities, but He got Abraham's nephew Lot out beforehand. What we learn here, however, is that God is not offended if you go to Him with an honest concern. He will work with you just like He worked with Abraham.

In Exodus, chapter 3, we read about Moses taking issue with something God told him to do. God went to Moses and told him to tell Pharaoh, "Let My people go."

The first thing Moses did was argue with Him! He said, "Lord, you have the wrong man."

God said, "I think not."

Moses said, "Lord, I don't speak well."

And the Lord said, "Well, I'll send Aaron your brother with you. He can do the talking."

Then Moses said, "But, Lord, who will I tell them sent me."

God answered, "Tell them I AM sent you!"

Finally, Moses ran out of objections.

There are many instances in the Bible when people challenged God and they were not always saying the right things, but He never seemed to be troubled by it. God got angry only when they talked to others in unbelief, doubt, criticism, or murmuring and complaining. God wants you to come to Him, talk to Him, and inquire of Him to get your answers.

Let me encourage you. As you change your conversation and modify what you say to line up with your rights of ownership in Jesus Christ, things may not change right away. In fact, as you confess to possess what is legally yours, it may make you feel really uncomfortable. You may even become frustrated when you put your faith out there, act upon it, and then nothing seems to happen when you think it will happen. But don't complain to your prayer partners. Don't criticize your pastor to your family or neighbors. Go directly to the Lord first. Seek His wisdom and counsel. Then, if you need counsel from others who are older in the Lord, go to them with a teachable spirit. Don't let fear and frustration stop you from possessing what is yours by saying things that mean, "It is vain to serve the Lord."

The Lord will be patient with you if you will be honest with Him. He's not hard to get along with! He is longsuffering, compassionate, and full of wisdom. He wants to fix the problems in your life. Jesus showed us that in Luke 13 when He said, "This is not the way things ought to be," and healed the crippled woman. He will help you get things to the way they ought to be.

When all is said and done, God is the only One who can help you. He is the only One who knows what's really going on and why you have not possessed what is rightfully yours. Taking your problems and complaints to other people instead of the Lord can only delay or stop you in possessing what you have been confessing. Instead, just go to God and say, "Lord, I need some help. It's just not working. I mean, it doesn't seem to be. I know what the Bible says, but I'm struggling, and obviously You couldn't be wrong! I must be doing something wrong, so show me what it is because I am determined not to quit. But the bill collectors are knocking on the door. They are calling on the phone. I need Your help now."

If you need human intervention, God will lead you to the person who's got the right answer for you. God will be quick to point you in the right direction and make the right connections for you. He'll tell you what you need to change in what you're thinking, what you're saying, or what you're doing. Remember, He says in James 1:5 that when we lack wisdom, all we need to do is ask Him, and He will tell us what we need to know.

CHAPTER 10

The Last Word

The LORD said unto Abram, after that Lot was separated from him, Lift up now thine eyes, and look from the place where thou art northward, and southward, and eastward, and westward:
For all the land which thou seest, to thee will I give it, and to thy seed for ever.

Genesis 13:14-15

You must possess by faith what God says you own. In this passage of Scripture, He gave Abram a promise. He didn't say He had already given the land to him and his descendants. He said, "to thee *will* I give it, and to thy seed for ever." At this point He hadn't given it yet. In chapter 15 of Genesis, when God made a covenant with Abram, He geographically defined the land that He had given to him and his descendants.

In the same day the LORD made a covenant with Abram, saying, Unto thy seed have I given this land, from the river of Egypt unto the great river, the river Euphrates:

Genesis 15:18

In this verse God used the past tense, saying, "Unto thy seed *have* I given this land." Later God changes Abram's name to Abraham and tells him again that the land of Canaan is his.

> *As for me, behold, my covenant is with thee, and thou shalt be a father of many nations.*
>
> *Neither shall thy name any more be called Abram, but thy name shall be Abraham; for a father of many nations have I made thee.*
>
> *And I will make thee exceeding fruitful, and I will make nations of thee, and kings shall come out of thee.*
>
> *And I will establish my covenant between me and thee and thy seed after thee in their generations for an everlasting covenant, to be a God unto thee, and to thy seed after thee.*
>
> *And I will give unto thee, and to thy seed after thee, the land wherein thou art a stranger, all the land of Canaan, for an everlasting possession; and I will be their God.*
>
> Genesis 17:4-8

God made a covenant with Abraham and said, "I will establish My covenant with you and your descendants for an everlasting covenant, and all the land of Canaan is yours for an everlasting possession." He also told Abraham in Genesis 15:13-16 that his descendants would be enslaved in a strange land, Egypt, but that they would return to the land of Canaan to possess it. The Word of God was passed down through the generations of Abraham's descendants, including Moses, Joshua, and Caleb. Moses led the children of Israel out of Egypt, and just before Joshua led them back into Canaan to possess it, God said the same thing to Joshua that He had said to Abraham.

Again, He spoke in past tense instead of future tense, saying "I have given unto you…"

> Every place that the sole of your foot shall tread upon, that have I given unto you, as I said unto Moses.
> From the wilderness and this Lebanon even unto the great river, the river Euphrates, all the land of the Hittites, and unto the great sea toward the going down of the sun, shall be your coast.
>
> Joshua 1:3-4

Legally the land was already theirs because of the covenant God had made with Abraham. He told Joshua what legally belonged to him and to all the descendants of Abraham. The land was theirs because He had already given it to them, but they had to possess it. That's why they called it "the Land of Promise." It had already been promised to them, but now they had to possess it.

Joshua led them across the Jordan River and they took Jericho, they defeated the giants, and they fought to possess what God had given them. By this time they were known as the children of Israel, so the land they possessed was called Israel. Unfortunately, as the years went by they stopped serving God, and their disobedience caused them to be taken into captivity by the Persians. After seventy years they were allowed to go back to their land. Then, after the crucifixion of Jesus, the Romans destroyed Jerusalem and drove most of them out of Israel again.

For centuries the land of Israel was occupied by foreign powers and Jewish people were scattered throughout the world. Then, in the late 1800s Jewish people began to return to Israel a few at a time. After World War II and the experience of the Holocaust, many went back to Israel and began to cry for a Jewish homeland to be reestablished. In 1948 Israel became a nation again. But it wasn't the United Nations or Britain or America that gave them the land. It was God who gave the land to their father Abraham and to his descendants thousands of years earlier. And God's promise still stands today.

Since 1948 the Israelis have had to fight to survive and keep their land. Israel has always been surrounded by large countries that are their enemies, who want to destroy them forever. Yet they continue to stand and fight decade after decade to stay there. Why? Because God gave them the land! They know what is legally theirs, and therefore they have the faith to remain there. God gave it to them and God will enable them to keep it as long as they serve Him.

If Israelis can stand on the promise of God year after year, through war and terrorism and all kinds of hardship, believers certainly should be able to possess their inheritance.

Who Is Greater in Your Eyes?

One night I was watching a documentary on the Arab-Israeli conflict in the Middle East. It was viewing the situation from the viewpoint of Egypt and Syria, and they interviewed their military leaders in the Six-Day War in 1973. An Egyptian general said, "We had been looking at the Israeli commanders since 1967. We knew what they could do, and we knew what we could do. And that land was ours."

When he said that, the Holy Ghost took me to what Jesus had said in Matthew, chapter 12. In the synagogue He had just cast a demon out of a man who had been dumb and blind.

> When the unclean spirit is gone out of a man, he walketh through dry places, seeking rest, and findeth none.
> Then he saith, I will return into my house [the devil said that; that's what the unclean spirit said] from whence I came out; and when he is come, he findeth it empty, swept, and garnished.
> Then goeth he, and taketh with himself seven other spirits more wicked than himself, and they enter in and dwell there: and the last state of that man is worse than the first. Even so shall it be also unto this wicked generation.
>
> Matthew 12:43-45

The devil who had been cast out called the man he had possessed, "my house." And that Egyptian general was calling Israel "his land." I began to see that even the devil knows that you possess what you confess! So I asked the following question: If two people believe they own the same thing and both confess their belief to possess it, who will get it?

In the case of the man in Matthew, chapter 12, we learn that the devil really believes we are his house to dwell in. Even after we are born again and the Holy Spirit inhabits us, the devil will continually try to take control of our lives, like we belong to him. But God says we are *His* house. What we are dealing with here is a territory dispute. The devil really believes he is going to win, just like the Egyptian general believed Israel was their land and they were going to take it. But they didn't.

Egypt did not take the land of Israel because they did not have a covenant with God or believe what the Bible says, which is that God had given the land to Abraham and his descendants. Without knowledge of and belief in the Word of God, the Egyptians were deceived by the enemy into thinking the land was theirs. Although they confessed that they possessed it, their words failed because God's Word is the greater authority. The earth is His and He gives it to whomever He pleases (Acts 17:26). None of the Arab nations have a legal claim on the land of Israel because God gave it to Abraham and his descendants.

The truth is, the enemy believes what he says and he can be very convincing. He can provide a lot of physical evidence to try to prove that the Word of God is not true for you in your life. That is why you need to know what God's Word really says and settle in your heart to stay with it, no matter what's going on in your life.

It's A Legal Matter

Your life is hid with Christ in God.

Colossians 3:3

As a born-again believer you are hid in Jesus. You belong to God and the devil has no legal claim on your spirit, soul, or body. You are the temple of the Lord, and Satan's evil influence has been replaced by the comfort, guidance, and teaching of the Spirit of God, who lives in your spirit. Jesus abides in you and you abide in Him, and He is Lord of ALL. Nevertheless, the devil still believes he has rights of ownership.

Sometimes the devil gains some territory in the lives of people and totally occupies them. When that is the case, we may say that person is demon *possessed* or *possessed* of the devil. The devil is always working to possess the territory that he has been evicted from. He is working to bring back all his works: Sickness. Disease. Lack. Fear. Pain. Depression. That's how he rules. But your life and entire outcome depends on what you choose to believe and say.

God says you belong to Him. You are bought with a price. Now the question is: Who will you walk with? You are the one in the middle who decides from moment to moment whether you will believe the lies of the devil or the truth of God's Word. You are the one who has the say about what you are going to possess and what's going to possess you. Jesus gave us a great example to follow in Luke, chapter 4, when He repeatedly defeated the devil with, "It is written...." When the devil went to Jesus in the wilderness and tempted Him in an effort to bring Jesus under his subjection and rule, he thought Jesus would submit to his lies and deception, just as Adam and Eve did in the Garden of Eden. But Jesus overcame every temptation by using the Word of God, saying, "It is written...." The devil and his attempts to control Jesus and all believers are no match for the Word of God, spoken from a heart of faith and love.

When Jesus used the phrase, "It is written...," He was speaking in legal terms. When you go to a court of law over a land dispute, whoever has the written deed to the land wins. When attorneys argue a case in court, they will refer to what is written either in the Constitution, case law, or specific legal documents that prove their client's claim. "Your Honor, I have this precedent. It is written in such-and-such case in Alabama...." Attorneys know that what is written is the deciding factor.

Attorneys don't wear chain mail armor and joust with one another before the judge and jury. They don't fight with swords or shoot it out with pistols. They argue their case with words. And when the judge makes his ruling, words are spoken that decree and finalize the outcome. Words are the weapons of the legal system in our country, and so it is with the Kingdom of God. Words are the legal weapons of our warfare. That's why Ephesians 6:17 calls the Word of God the sword of the Spirit.

The spoken Word of God carries power because God's Word is the supreme legal authority in the universe. His Word is the LAST WORD on every subject and every dispute. And there is no higher authority to whom you can appeal. When God has spoken, your outcome is decreed!

When Satan went to tempt Jesus in the wilderness, to bring Him under his evil control and thwart the plan of God, Jesus dealt with him on a legal basis. He spoke God's Word, "It is written…," and thereby He gave you and me the pattern to follow whenever the devil comes to us to steal, kill, or destroy any area of our lives. When the bills are piled up and Satan tempts you to complain, despair, or commit a crime, just say, "It is written that God supplies all my need according to His riches in glory by Christ Jesus" (Philippians 4:19). When the doctor gives you a bad report and the devil feeds you thoughts of fear, pain, and death, boldly confess, "It is written that Jesus bore my sickness and disease, with His stripes I am healed, and with long life He will satisfy me" (Matthew 8:17; 1 Peter 2:24; Psalm 91:16).

By faith in God and His Word we possess and continue to hold what He has given us, just like the children of Israel possessed and continue to hold the Promised Land. The final authority in any trial, test, or attack is always the spoken Word of God. As you speak God's Word with the authority He has given you, you will possess and maintain your inheritance.

CHAPTER 11

Faith and Your Authority

As joint-heirs with Jesus we have been given the authority to do something about situations that are not as they ought to be. In Jesus' name we have authority to preach the Gospel, make disciples, heal the sick, cast out demons, feed and clothe the poor, and literally change the lives of those whose lives are not as they ought to be.

We have a commission from Jesus to make a difference wherever we go. We have a divine responsibility to use the authority He has given us in our lives for the benefit of ourselves and others. We're not to just sit on our hands and watch things go wrong and do nothing. We Americans especially are richly blessed, and as a country that has operated primarily on Christian values and ideals, we have done more to help other nations than any other country in history. Even as a country, when we see that things are not as they ought to be, we step in and change things for the better.

The devil and his world systems would have you believe that everybody is unique, every case is different, and things are not always black and white. You may hear someone say, "There's a lot of gray area in this situation." While it's true that we should judge each situation on its own merits, there is right and wrong. There are evil thoughts and behavior and righteous thoughts and behavior. And when you encounter something that is wrong or evil, don't be afraid to call it what it is.

Jesus in Me Makes Me Greater

God, who at sundry times and in divers manners spake in time past unto the fathers by the prophets,

Hath in these last days spoken unto us by his Son, whom he hath appointed heir of all things, by whom also he made the worlds;

Who being the brightness of his glory, and the express image of his person, and upholding all things by the word of his power, when he had by himself purged our sins, sat down on the right hand of the Majesty on high:

Being made so much better than the angels, as he hath by inheritance obtained a more excellent name than they.

For unto which of the angels said he at any time, Thou art my Son, this day have I begotten thee? And again, I will be to him a Father, and he shall be to me a Son?

But to which of the angels said he at any time, Sit on my right hand, until I make thine enemies thy footstool?

Are they not all ministering spirits, sent forth to minister for them who shall be heirs of salvation?

Hebrews 1:1-5,13-14

When we read this passage of Scripture in light of faith and our authority in Jesus Christ, we can see another facet of who we are and what we have in Him. We know that Satan was once Lucifer the archangel, a magnificent creature who ruled the earth. Nevertheless, he wasn't the brightest bulb in the chandelier. Not only did he turn against God and try to overthrow Him, but after God soundly defeated him, he continued to believe he could still beat God, destroy mankind, and rule the earth again. He has to be crazy to think that way, but the Bible says that he is the father of lies, so he must believe his own lies.

When God made Adam and Eve and gave them dominion over the earth, Satan made his first move to get control of them and thus get control of the earth. And since that time in the Garden of Eden when Adam and Eve yielded their authority to him, Satan has asserted himself in the affairs of human beings, and it has always been an ownership dispute. Even though Jesus soundly defeated him, stripping him of all authority and dominion, Satan still thinks he owns this planet and those who live here. He thinks he can do as he pleases in the earth, and many times he gets away with it. It is up to the body of Christ to dethrone him and take our seats in the place of authority that Jesus provided.

God, who is rich in mercy, for his great love wherewith he loved us,
Even when we were dead in sins, hath quickened us together with
Christ, (by grace ye are saved;)
And hath raised us up together, and made us sit together in heav-
enly places in Christ Jesus.

Ephesians 2:4-6

We are sitting with Jesus at the right hand of the Most High God, who is our Father. We are joint-heirs with Jesus Christ. God makes Satan Jesus' footstool, and He makes Satan our footstool. According to Hebrews 1:14, God's angels are ministering spirits sent forth to minister to the heirs of salvation. That's us! We are the heirs of salvation, and the angels are to serve us.

You should have no doubt that Jesus is superior to Satan in every respect. He is superior to him in glory. He is superior to him in intelligence. He is superior to him in anointing and power. He is superior to him in God-given authority. He is superior to him as a being, being the only begotten Son of God. And He is superior to Satan in legal rights of ownership.

Giving thanks unto the Father, which hath made us meet to be
partakers of the inheritance of the saints in light:
Who hath delivered us from the power of darkness, and hath
translated us into the kingdom of his dear Son:
In whom we have redemption through his blood, even the forgive-
ness of sins:
Who is the image of the invisible God, the firstborn of every creature:

For by him were all things created, that are in heaven, and that are in earth, visible and invisible, whether they be thrones, or dominions, or principalities, or powers: all things were created by him, and for him:

And he is before all things, and by him all things consist.

Colossians 1:12-17

Jesus created all things, including Lucifer, and that makes Jesus superior because He is the Creator and Lucifer is the creation. This passage in Colossians also says that God made us "partakers of the inheritance of the saints in light." Acts 17:28 says, "For in him we live, and move, and have our being;...For we are also his offspring." You can't get any more "one with God" than being "in Him." Therefore, as children of God we are also superior to Satan in every respect. We have ownership rights that are superior to Satan's because we abide in Jesus, who created everything and owns everything.

When it comes to dealing with Satan and his demons, we should be declaring that planet earth is *our* planet! Christians ought to believe the world is ours, that we own it. I'm not talking about taking other people's property or oppressing people. I'm talking about operating in the spiritual authority we have been given in Christ Jesus over all the power of the enemy, taking authority over him and his demons whenever they rear their ugly heads in the affairs of those around us and in our individual lives.

The Good Fight of Faith

Fight the good fight of faith, lay hold on eternal life, whereunto thou art also called, and hast professed a good profession before many witnesses.

1 Timothy 6:12

The Bible says that the fight of faith is a good fight, that we are called to "lay hold" or possess all that eternal life gives us, and that when we profess faith it is a good profession to other people who hear us.

The question now arises: What are you fighting for? According to the Word of God you are not fighting for ownership. You are fighting to possess what you already own in Christ Jesus. You are fighting to possess what is legally yours and to keep what is legally yours. You can look to the children of Israel as an example. When God told Joshua to take the Promised Land in Joshua, chapter 1, the Canaanites had lived there for hundreds of years. This is a picture of how the devil and his demons have oppressed and dominated you, your family, your community, your nation, mankind, and this planet for years. But there is no such thing as "squatters' rights" in God's Kingdom. Just because the devil has been there for years doesn't mean he has a legal right to stay there.

God has given you your inheritance. Now it's up to you to kick the devil out of your life and possess all He has for you! Like Joshua, you need to cross the Jordan and attack lack, sickness, depression, and all manner of sin or bondage that hinders you in your walk with the Lord. Like the Canaanites, the devil will think the land belongs to him. He will try to convince you that you have no rights or authority over lack, sickness, depression, or any of his arsenal of sin and bondage. That's when you pull out your covenant—the New Covenant in the blood of Jesus—and your title deed of faith to inform the enemy that he's too late. God's Word is your evidence of things you own, even if you have not yet seen them. You have inherited all things pertaining to life and godliness. Jesus obtained it, you know it's yours, and now you are confessing it to possess it.

Probably the biggest reason Christians live below their inheritance in Jesus is that they refuse to deal with the enemy. They don't want to fight for it or are content to just drift along in life, attributing everything that happens to them as being God's will. Satan can run right over this type of Christian. But their lives would change dramatically if they would just stop determining God's will by their circumstances and start discovering God's will from His Word! Not only that, their lives would bring glory to God as they demonstrated His faithfulness.

God has set us in a place of ownership and told us to possess our inheritance. He's told us we have an enemy and has given us clear instructions how to deal with him. We can look to Jesus, the Author and Finisher of our faith, and follow His example. Jesus defeated the devil, saying, "It is written." Then

He gave us His name, His power of attorney, and told us to defeat the devil the same way (Mark 16:17).

We talk about our authority as believers. Authority is a legal term, and the highest authority is always in control. When a crime is committed, the local sheriff on the scene takes control of the situation. But then he discovers the crime goes beyond his jurisdiction when the state troopers come in and take control. They figure out that the perpetrator has crossed state lines and now it's a federal crime. Suddenly the FBI shows up and they take control. That is always the way it works, both in natural matters and in spiritual matters. When multiple authorities are present, the highest authority will claim jurisdiction and take control.

Local and state authorities may not give up their jurisdiction easily. The FBI has got to have legal evidence that they have jurisdiction because a lower authority doesn't like being pushed out of the way even if they are on the same side. But if they are on opposite sides in a jurisdiction dispute, like Satan is with believers, they will always resist being shut down and kicked out of a territory they consider to be theirs. When you encounter this kind of resistance, stand firm! You are backed by the highest power in the universe and are using the name that is above every other name. You have a legal, written document to back you up. All you have to do is say, "It is written…," and there is nothing the enemy can do to stop you from fully possessing what is yours.

It All Begins With You

Possession begins with understanding your rights of ownership, but let's take this a little deeper. It's not just knowing what you have that will keep your faith steadfast and enable you to possess what God has for you; it's knowing *who you are in Him.* Remember, your faith is rooted and grounded in God's love for you. You must never lose sight of the fact that you are His beloved child, and He has withheld no good thing from you.

The first thing you have to possess is YOU, your identity in Christ. Without that you will have no faith-legs to stand on and will be unable to possess anything else. If you are born of God, then you are a child of God. Any thought that opposes that truth is a lie of the enemy that needs to be eliminated from your thinking entirely. There is a great example of what I'm talking about in the Old Testament.

> *The LORD spake unto Moses in the plains of Moab by Jordan near Jericho, saying,*
> *Speak unto the children of Israel, and say unto them, When ye are passed over Jordan into the land of Canaan;*
> *Then ye shall drive out all the inhabitants of the land from before you, and destroy all their pictures, and destroy all their molten images, and quite pluck down all their high places:*
> *And ye shall dispossess the inhabitants of the land, and dwell therein: for I have given you the land to possess it.*
>
> Numbers 33:50-53

God said, "The enemy is in your houses, eating your crops, driving your cars, and making your children wild. Kick them out! Dispossess them. I have given you the land to possess."

If ye will not drive out the inhabitants of the land from before you; then it shall come to pass, that those which ye let remain of them shall be pricks in your eyes, and thorns in your sides, and shall vex you in the land wherein ye dwell.

Moreover it shall come to pass, that I shall do unto you, as I thought to do unto them.

Numbers 33:55-56

Whatever you don't drive out of your life will be a problem to you for the rest of your life. Kick out any doubt and unbelief, carnality, or sin that you have allowed to operate in your life— especially wrong thinking and wrong attitudes about yourself. Renew your mind continually with God's Word to eradicate small-mindedness, seeing yourself as unworthy, unable, and under the condemnation of sin. God wants you to see yourself as righteous and able to do whatever He tells you to do because you live and move and have your being in Him (Acts 17:28). He wants you to dream big and go after it, to possess the dreams He has put in your heart instead of talking or worrying yourself out of them. Purge yourself of all unscriptural thinking and bring your flesh under control by driving it out with God's Word. Moses is a perfect example of someone who failed to do this, and it cost him dearly.

The people thirsted there for water; and the people murmured against Moses, and said, Wherefore is this that thou hast brought us up out of Egypt, to kill us and our children and our cattle with thirst?

And Moses cried unto the LORD, saying, What shall I do unto this people? they be almost ready to stone me.

And the LORD said unto Moses, Go on before the people, and take with thee of the elders of Israel; and thy rod, wherewith thou smotest the river, take in thine hand, and go.

Behold, I will stand before thee there upon the rock in Horeb; and thou shalt smite the rock, and there shall come water out of it, that the people may drink. And Moses did so in the sight of the elders of Israel.

Exodus 17:3-6

The people needed water, and when Moses obeyed God and hit the rock, water came out of it. In case you don't think this is a very big deal, stop and consider how much water had to flow out of that rock to quench the thirst of more than a million Israelites and all their herds of sheep and cattle.

In Numbers, chapter 20, history repeats itself, with one significant difference. Again the children of Israel cried for water. And again Moses sought God's help, only this time God altered His instructions to Moses.

Take the rod, and gather thou the assembly together, thou, and Aaron thy brother, and speak ye unto the rock before their eyes; and it shall give forth his water, and thou shalt bring forth to them

water out of the rock: so thou shalt give the congregation and their
beasts drink.

Numbers 20:8

Instead of striking the rock to bring forth water, God told
Moses to *speak* to the rock. But by now, Moses was really fed up
with the people and their whining. He had stood up to Pharaoh
numerous times to get the people delivered from their bondage
in Egypt, and time after time God had proved Himself with
miracles like parting the Red Sea, drowning Pharaoh's armies,
and supernaturally providing for them and preserving them.
Now, again, they had nothing good to say about Moses and even
tried to stone him. Moses had heard enough of their complaining, and instead of speaking to the rock, he angrily hit it.

> *Moses took the rod from before the LORD, as he commanded him.*
> *And Moses and Aaron gathered the congregation together before*
> *the rock, and he said unto them, Hear now, ye rebels; must we*
> *fetch you water out of this rock?*
> *And Moses lifted up his hand, and with his rod he smote the rock*
> *twice: and the water came out abundantly, and the congregation*
> *drank, and their beasts also.*
> *And the LORD spake unto Moses and Aaron, Because ye believed*
> *me not, to sanctify me in the eyes of the children of Israel, there-*
> *fore ye shall not bring this congregation into the land which I have*
> *given them.*

Numbers 20:9-12

Moses disobeyed the Word of God. Instead of following God's instruction and speaking to the rock, he struck the rock like he had before. Why? Because he had never dealt with his anger. His anger caused him to disobey God's instructions. As a result, God told him that he would not lead the people into the Promised Land.

The reason Moses did not get to lead Israel into the Promised Land was not because he was too old and God wanted somebody younger or because he had fulfilled his assignment. Moses did not go in because he disobeyed God by not speaking His Word. What a shame to get to the end of the road and miss out on possessing the biggest thing in human history all because your flesh had not been dealt with and you didn't speak what God told you to speak. Unfortunately, this happens every day to Christians whom God has given a great inheritance, a great destiny, and all His blessings. Instead of speaking the Word of God and possessing what He has for them, they get angry and offended and never declare His Word.

What you confess you possess, and that includes YOU!

Wouldn't it be a shame to fall short of God's promise to you just because you didn't speak? Wouldn't it be a shame to fall short of your healing just because you didn't declare it is yours? Wouldn't it be a shame to fall short of the abundance and the overflow God promises in His Word just because you didn't feel like fighting for it?

Few Fights Are Won With the First Punch

Ye shall serve the LORD your God, and he shall bless thy bread, and thy water; and I will take sickness away from the midst of thee.

There shall nothing cast their young, nor be barren, in thy land: the number of thy days I will fulfil.

I will send my fear before thee, and will destroy all the people to whom thou shalt come, and I will make all thine enemies turn their backs unto thee.

And I will send hornets before thee, which shall drive out the Hivite, the Canaanite, and the Hittite, from before thee.

I will not drive them out from before thee in one year; lest the land become desolate, and the beast of the field multiply against thee.

By little and little I will drive them out from before thee, until thou be increased, and inherit the land.

And I will set thy bounds from the Red sea even unto the sea of the Philistines, and from the desert unto the river: for I will deliver the inhabitants of the land into your hand; and thou shalt drive them out before thee.

Exodus 23:25-31

God is illustrating a very important principle in this passage of Scripture. When you speak the Word, when you confess what He wants you to possess, you probably are not going to get it all at once. Just like a prize fighter, you are going to win by throwing one punch at a time, one after another. It is rare that a boxer will step into the ring and knock out his opponent with the first punch, and so it is with possessing your inheritance.

You will possess your inheritance step by step, blow by blow, as you speak and walk in faith and drive out the enemy. You are going to have to keep walking in faith. You are going to have to keep confessing to possess what is yours. You are going to have to enforce God's will in your life, keep your flesh in subjection, believe God's Word over circumstances and feelings, and as you do you will possess all that God has provided.

To fight the good fight of faith, you must never give up. Stay in God's Word and keep your faith fired up. Speak God's Word over your situation. Don't complain to anyone; go to God when things don't go the way you thought they would. Settle your questions and disputes with Him, and continue speaking His Word in faith. Every time you confess the Word, you are taking steps to possess what God has given you.

CHAPTER 12

Slaying Your Giants of Fear

Now that you understand that God loves you and wants you to prosper and be in health in all areas of your life, what is the greatest obstacle in obtaining your inheritance? What do you think is the biggest hindrance to possessing the promises of God, the benefits of God, all to which you have rights of ownership?

Traditions of men?

Ignorance?

Religious mindsets?

Doubt and unbelief?

All these things can certainly get in the way of your possessing your inheritance from God, but there is one more that is worse than all of these: F-E-A-R.

James 2:20,26 says that faith without works is dead, so by faith you speak *and* act according to God's Word and the leading of the Holy Spirit. Like the woman with the spirit of infirmity, you walk forward to experience the healing touch of Jesus. Like the children of Israel, you cross the Jordan and defeat the enemy to possess what God has given you. Fear, on the other hand, freezes you. You can be paralyzed by fear, unable to move at all and your faith becomes of no effect.

Faith acts.

Fear freezes.

Not Facing Your Fear Brings Failure

What is the source of fear? Where does fear come from? The Bible shows us that fear is a tactic and device of the devil. It is a method he uses to intimidate Christians by magnifying the problems of life and making them appear as giants. Just like most of the children of Israel froze when they encountered the giants in the Promised Land, the devil wants Christians to freeze and do nothing because of their fear. But let's take another look at what happened to the children of Israel and see what we can learn.

God had brought them out of Egypt with all kinds of miracles and wonders. They had seen His delivering power again and again, but when they stood at the River Jordan and heard the two spies' good report and the ten spies' evil report, they chose to go with the evil report.

They told him, and said, We came unto the land whither thou sentest us, and surely it floweth with milk and honey; and this is the fruit of it.

Nevertheless the people be strong that dwell in the land, and the cities are walled, and very great: and moreover we saw the children of Anak there.

Numbers 13:27-28

Anak and his family were giants, and when the children of Israel heard that they were in the land they were going in to possess, they were horrified and cried out. Only Caleb and Joshua remained in faith.

Caleb stilled the people before Moses, and said, Let us go up at once, and possess it; for we are well able to overcome it.

Numbers 13:30

Caleb was ready to go! He and Joshua were so full of God's promise and the faith it ignited that they were chomping at the bit to possess what He had given them. That is how faith works. Faith acts. Faith rises up and compels us to act immediately in God's power and authority. If we stop to focus on how great the giants are instead of keeping our focus on the exceeding great and precious promises of God, fear will freeze us into doing nothing. Fear can cause us to delay or forfeit what God has promised.

The men that went up with him said, We be not able to go up against the people; for they are stronger than we.

And they brought up an evil report of the land which they had searched unto the children of Israel, saying, The land, through which we have gone to search it, is a land that eateth up the inhab-itants thereof; and all the people that we saw in it are men of a great stature.

And there we saw the giants, the sons of Anak, which come of the giants: and we were in our own sight as grasshoppers, and so we were in their sight.

Numbers 13:31-33

What was the biggest obstacle that these people faced? Many people would read this story and say that the biggest obstacle they faced was the giants, but the giants weren't really their problem. Their problem was what the giants inspired in them, which was fear. Fear affected how they saw themselves! Although the giants may have been more than a match for them, the giants were no match for God. The children of Israel forgot they weren't fighting to possess the land in their own power; they were going in under the banner of Almighty God and the authority of His Word.

Consider this: God was reaching into that land and using them to do it. These people were being used of God. As His army they were enforcing His will. They weren't out there on their own, praying that maybe they might stumble into His benefits. No! They were God's instruments of righteousness possessing their Promised Land. God had brought them out of Egypt, through the wilderness, to the Jordan River, and said, "I have given you the land. As I was with Moses, I will be with you. We are going to take this land together, and I'm going to work through you" (Joshua 1:1-8, my paraphrase).

Unfortunately, when the children of Israel heard about the sons of Anak, the giants who stood between them and the promise of God, they forgot who they were and what God had said! They forgot that when God tells you to do something, He is going to help you do it and it's going to bring blessing. There may be some things you have to work through and overcome, but in the end nothing makes you happier than obeying God and doing what He wants you to do.

The children of Israel forgot not only what God had promised, but also they forgot that God was with them. They stopped looking at Him, started looking at the giants, and what the giants inspired in them was fear. Instead of seeing themselves as God's covenant people, walking in the legal authority and power of Almighty God, they saw themselves as grasshoppers. They compared themselves to the giants instead of comparing the giants to God. So they stopped, froze, and failed. Because of fear they never entered the Promised Land.

If you face and overcome your fears, you will see yourself as you really are—a champion, a child of the Most High God! But if you don't face and overcome your fears, you'll never see yourself as God sees you and become who He says you are. Then the devil will use your fears to keep you bound, forgetting who you are, whose you are, and what you have in Jesus. He will put giants in your path, those things that bring fear to your heart, to divert your attention from the promises and power of God. If you give in to it instead of defeating it, fear will always paralyze you and steal your faith and vision.

That generation of the children of Israel never faced and therefore never overcame their fear of giants. They didn't even fight the giants. We can't say that the giants kept them out of the Promised Land because the giants didn't defeat them. What defeated them was the FEAR of fighting the giants. They died not knowing whether they could have defeated them or not, and they forfeited their inheritance because they never tried.

Faith Acts at Once

Joshua and Caleb had the answer to dealing with giants of fear. They said, "Let us go up at once, and possess it; for we are well able to overcome it" (Numbers 13:30). *The key to overcoming the fear of giants is to tackle them immediately.* Don't give yourself any time to worry and compare yourself with that big oaf. The more you sit around and think about facing him, the bigger he will become and the greater the fear will become. Go when you've got Holy Ghost momentum. If you're taking steps to possess what God has promised you and you encounter a giant of fear, don't stop. Go up at once and kill it before it kills your dreams, your hopes, and your destiny.

I'm going to be straight with you. Once you step out in faith to possess what God has provided in His Word, you may not encounter only one giant; you may have to deal with his whole family! But do you think it's any harder for you and God to overcome a hundred giants than it is one? Nothing is impossible with our God, and "all things are possible to him that believeth" (Mark 9:23). When you go at once in God's power, it doesn't matter how many giants are in your path. Just obey God's instructions to Joshua and "be thou strong and very courageous" (Joshua 1:7). Trust God and you will win the battle!

David is another person in the Bible who faced some giants. Most everyone knows the story told in 1 Samuel, chapter 17. David was just a young man bringing food to his older brothers, who were soldiers on the battlefield. When he arrived, the first thing he heard were the taunting words of a giant named Goliath, issuing a challenge to Israel to fight him. When no one accepted his challenge, Goliath stood there day after day and mocked all of Israel. This had gone on for weeks, and by the time David arrived the whole army was terrified. Fear had paralyzed them, and all they could talk about was how big and dreadful their enemy was. Even King Saul, who had been a man of valor in battle before, sat in his tent and asked, "Do we have any volunteers?"

David took one look at Goliath and said, "Let me at him!" He did that because he knew God was bigger than any giant he faced. God had already helped him kill a lion and a bear that had tried to take the sheep he was tending. By the time he encountered Goliath, he was almost cocky with faith in God.

When David heard Goliath's words, he reacted differently than the soldiers. He knew the power of words, and that God's Word was superior to anyone else's words, including a giant's. Remember, words are the weapons of law in the courtroom. The accuser of the brethren attacks us with words, and we use God's Word with His authority and power to defeat him. David understood this. When he heard Goliath's challenge, he fought back with words.

> *Who is this uncircumcised Philistine, that he should defy the armies of the living God?*
>
> 1 Samuel 17:26

David knew this was no time to sit around and analyze the situation or fear would get a grip on him too. He knew the time to act was right at that moment, so he went immediately to Saul and said, "I'll fight the giant." Also, by calling the giant an "uncircumcised Philistine," he declared that this was a covenant battle because circumcision was the seal of Israel's covenant with God. David knew God would deliver him because he was in covenant with Him.

Practice, Practice, Practice

When David volunteered to fight Goliath, Saul agreed to let David go out against him, even though he noticed that David was pretty young. He probably felt a little guilty, like he was feeding David to the wolves, so he offered him his armor.

David may have thought, *If your armor is so good, if it's the answer, why haven't you strapped it on and gone out to fight with it?* But out of respect for the king, he tried the armor and saw that it didn't fit him. He said, "This is not me," and took it off. He wanted to fight with the weapons he had proved and knew would work.

David was a superior warrior, first because he didn't allow fear to freeze him, and second because he knew what worked for him. He had fought a lion and a bear, and his experience told him what was best to fight the giant. His experience with God's power and faithfulness were what David depended on.

As children of God, we all need practice in defeating the giants that come up against us. We all need to exercise our faith whenever we can and get used to using the weapons of our warfare. If we never exercise our faith and we wait until a giant shows up, we are more apt to freeze and flee. But if we have practiced with the lion and the bear and have experience under our belts, we are more likely to act quickly and boldly when a giant shows up.

When you are just beginning to exercise your faith and prove God's faithfulness, start out believing for something small, just to learn and get some practice. I heard a man say once, "Believe God for shoestrings before you believe Him for an airplane." That's good advice! Start with something you need and believe God until you get it.

I know a man who liked a certain kind of doughnuts, and he didn't have any money to buy them, so he started using his faith by asking God for doughnuts. When he got to work, somebody came in and gave him a box of doughnuts! You would have thought they had given him the whole store, because that's how it feels when you step out in faith and God comes through for you. That's how you get some experience under your belt and prove your faith in God. You learn the particular ways God wants to work through you to defeat the enemy and possess what He's given you. Then, once you possess some things, become skilled with your faith, and taste victory, you will never want to turn and run again.

Even if you haven't used your faith for a while, the skill you gained through years of practice and experience will come back by God's grace. I mentioned earlier in this book that I used to be in law enforcement and was trained and experienced with firearms. I used to be a pretty good shot back then because my life and my partner's life may have depended on it. Anyway, years later I came across an indoor shooting range, and I decided to stop in. I bought a silhouette target and also a target of a guy wearing a stocking cap and sunglasses, holding a woman in front of him and pointing a gun at her head. The idea was that he was holding her hostage.

Shooting ranges like this have individual stalls with dividers. You stand in your stall, hook up your target, and then send it out as far as you want it to go. Everyone else on the range can see your target and where your bullets hit it. There were about five or six lanes, and I went all the way to the wall. I first shot at the silhouette, running it out different distances, and I was doing really well. Eventually I put up the hostage target, and I'll tell you the truth, that criminal would not have wanted to be up against me! I hit him right in the nose and didn't even come close to hitting the woman. Several other shooters noticed and came over to say, "That's good shooting!"

It felt good to know that I hadn't lost the skill I had gained through years of practice. When you practice until you master something, even if you don't use it for a while, it will come back to you when you need it. This is an important principle in spiritual things as well as natural things. Use your faith and go shoot something! Blow some giant away! Believe God for something new. Study the Scriptures, meditate on the Word, confess the Word, and begin to act like it is true—because it is. Get those faith fundamentals down, and before you know it, somebody will say, "Wow, that's good shooting!"

Practice using your faith the same way an athlete practices before a big game or event. Get your faith in shape, be familiar with how it works, and be ready to face the challenge. David practiced on the lion and the bear, and it paid off. By the time he faced Goliath he knew what worked for him. Without hesitation he got his sling and went over to the brook to pick out five smooth stones.

Power of Attorney

When Goliath saw David coming out against him, he began to mock him and curse him. He saw that David was young and small, so he insulted him and the Israelites in order to intimidate this kid they had sent out.

> *The Philistine said unto David, Am I a dog, that thou comest to me with staves? And the Philistine cursed David by his gods.*
>
> 1 Samuel 17:43

Why was the giant saying these things? He was trying to inspire fear in David. He was trying to terrify him because he was a warrior who understood that if you can frighten your enemies, you've already got them 90 percent defeated. But David had already overcome the growl of the bear and the roar of the lion by the power of God. He was not intimidated by Goliath's taunting words, and he yelled right back at him.

> *Then said David to the Philistine, Thou comest to me with a sword, and with a spear, and with a shield: but I come to thee in the name of the LORD of hosts, the God of the armies of Israel, whom thou hast defied.*
>
> 1 Samuel 17:45

David didn't know His Name, but he was talking about Jesus, the Lord of hosts and the God of the armies of Israel. We face all our giants in the Name of Jesus because His Name is a legal term in the courts of the universe. He has given us His

Name to use to do His will in the earth. In today's legal system, they call that "power of attorney." If my friend gives me power of attorney over his financial affairs, then I can go to his bank and use his name to withdraw the funds I need to pay his bills or whatever else needs to be done. If I haven't been given the authority to use his name, all my bluff and bravado won't cash a check. But if I've got power of attorney from him, then I can access whatever is in his account to do my job for him.

Jesus gave us His Name so that we could carry out His business until He returned. We are His body, His ambassadors, and His representatives on this earth. He also gave us His Name to overcome any fear that rises up to stop us, to defeat any giants who are trying to terrify us and to keep us from possessing what legally belongs to Him and us. Remember, we are joint-heirs with Jesus. He's given us His Name, His power of attorney, to possess *our* inheritance.

Speak the Word and Attack

If you ever wonder what to do in a situation, just ask yourself what Jesus would do. What would Jesus do if He was facing a giant? He wouldn't listen to his taunts and jeers, and He certainly wouldn't be afraid of him. Out of His mouth would come a sharp, two-edged sword and the giant would either run, surrender, or be killed. That's what happens when Jesus opens His mouth, and that's what happens when anyone in Him speaks the Word in faith as David did to Goliath.

This day will the LORD deliver thee into mine hand; and I will smite thee, and take thine head from thee; and I will give the carcases of the host of the Philistines this day unto the fowls of the air, and to the wild beasts of the earth; that all the earth may know that there is a God in Israel.

And all this assembly shall know that the LORD saveth not with sword and spear: for the battle is the LORD's, and he will give you into our hands.

1 Samuel 17:46-47

Notice David didn't say the Lord would deliver Goliath into his hand tomorrow or next month. He didn't say, "I'm coming back tomorrow to finish you off," or, "You just wait until Friday!" Why? Because he understood that you can't mess around with fear and the devil. The minute the giant appears and fear tries to take hold of your heart, you have to shoot it with the Word right then. If you wait until Friday, you or someone else in unbelief will talk you out of it, and fear will freeze you. That's why David said, "This day…"

The minute after David spoke the Word, he acted on the Word.

It came to pass, when the Philistine arose, and came and drew nigh to meet David, that David hastened, and ran toward the army to meet the Philistine.

1 Samuel 17:48

The Bible says David "hastened, and ran toward." He didn't sink down on his knees to pray or meditate about what he was about to do. He just did it. And the rest, as they say, is history.

As he ran he reached into his bag, pulled out a stone, slung it with a sling, and POW! Goliath hit the ground. David understood the principle, "Let us go up at once, and possess it" (Numbers 13:30).

Whatever fear stands in your way, charge it! Don't sit back and wait on God to kill it. He has given *you* the authority to kill it. You have Jesus' power of attorney to use His Name and His Word. Fear is not something that you can just outlast. Fear must to be attacked aggressively and immediately. Fear and the giants that inspire fear are like rattlesnakes that have crawled into your house. First you slay them with the sword of the Spirit, and then you find out how they got in and plug the holes with God's Word so they can't get back in.

We've all had symptoms that made us afraid. Some people are so afraid that they won't go to the doctor until things are so bad it's nearly impossible to keep their faith strong to be healed. Being afraid of a doctor's report is not walking in faith. It may just be your own thoughts and past experience taunting you and making you fearful that you might get a bad report. But even if you get a bad report, realize that a bad report is nothing more than the fear-inspiring words of a giant that needs to be shut up and evicted from your life.

Instead of being afraid of a bad report, attack it! If you are diagnosed with some kind of disease, learn all you can about it. Don't just ignore it and decide you simply won't think about it. That's fear! I've seen unbelievers educate themselves about their problem and figure out their path to healing either with their doctor's help or through some kind of alternative treatment. The reason they got well was because they attacked the disease instead of running from it in fear and dread. Don't be afraid to educate yourself about whatever giant you are facing. Most of the time, when you shine the light on it you'll find out that it's not as big as it seems.

The second thing you must do is focus your attention on the cure and not the disease. You have more going for you than an unbeliever because you are in close personal contact with the Healer, the Great Physician. The Holy Spirit will lead you into all truth, and that includes everything you need to know to defeat the giants in your life. Jesus is always the answer. He will tell you what you need to do spiritually, mentally, and physically to slay your giant.

Take Courage

When I was a kid I was ashamed any time I was afraid. I always felt like I was being less than a man if I was afraid. So when I was young I would just berate myself for feeling fear. Of course, it doesn't do any good to kick yourself around, and it never helped me. Later, when I got into the Word of God and began to understand how fear worked, I realized that there was something God had been trying to teach me all along.

First of all, feeling afraid is human. Everyone is afraid at one time or another. There is no shame in initially feeling afraid. God knows this, which is why He kept telling Joshua to be courageous and to meditate in His Word. He was teaching us that there is great honor and certain victory in facing your fears and overcoming them with your faith in Him and His Word.

God also showed me that instead of attacking myself for being afraid, He wanted me to attack my fears. I had always been afraid of swimming in deep water, so I took up scuba diving. It wasn't long before that fear was defeated in my life. I was afraid of heights, so I made myself climb water towers. When I was younger, I climbed every water tower in the county until I wasn't afraid of heights anymore.

You can face whatever giants of fear are holding you back and keeping you down, and the Holy Spirit will show you how to defeat them. Fear comes to everyone—fear of failure, fear of loneliness, fear of financial lack. Fear will attack almost any aspect of life, especially those areas of God's promise. That is because fear is Satan's main tactic to keep us bound and unable to fulfill what God has called us to do.

The devil will also use fear to get you on the wrong path or to take a turn you shouldn't take. We see this so many times in relationships between men and women. Women especially seem to fall prey to fear in this area of life. Some women will hold on to the worst relationships or even marry a total jerk just because they are afraid of being without a man. Instead of confronting the inconsistencies and things that they suspect are true about their man, like he's lying, he's selfish and self-centered, or worse, he's violent and abusive, they just stick their head in the sand and ignore the signs. They will keep that man in their lives, afraid the relationship will end if they confront these things— but that would be the best thing for them!

As long as they allow fear to rule their hearts instead of having faith and trusting God for the right person, that giant of fear will keep them out of God's will and on the wrong path. If they would turn to God and His Word, muster all their courage and faith, and charge that giant, they would find out he was nothing but mouth and bluff! It was all smoke and mirrors! Fear is just a magnifier that makes bad things look big. But the giants we are afraid of are nothing when we measure them against the Lord Jesus Christ!

Don't tolerate fear in any form, whether it's worry, uncertainty, anxiety, or just being nervous. Don't let any of these things get a foothold in your thoughts. If you've been ashamed of being afraid like I was, understand what God is saying to you today. It is not dishonorable to have fear, but it is dishonorable not to face it and overcome it. Whatever your giants are, with the guidance and power of the Holy Spirit in you and the authority of God's Word and the Name of Jesus backing you, you can take courage and defeat the giants of fear in your life.

CHAPTER 13

Catching the Spirit of Faith

Through the years I have watched people sit in the same church services, go to the same Bible school, hear the same teachers, and come up under the same mentors. Some will go out and accomplish great things for the Kingdom of God, while others always seem to be struggling. Some rise up and conquer in the face of adversity, while others move from one crisis to another, never realizing any success. These are people who have heard the Word of God, they have studied and seem to have applied faith in their circumstances, and yet they are unproductive in many or all areas of their lives. While others are blessed and moving from glory to glory, they stay the same or even go backwards.

Why is that? What makes the difference? I began to question the Lord about this. I wanted to understand why this was happening in order to help those who were floundering. The Holy Spirit led me to the answer in His Word.

We having the same spirit of faith, according as it is written, I believed, and therefore have I spoken; we also believe, and therefore speak.

2 Corinthians 4:13

When you were born again, God gave you the measure of faith. Faith is not just a subject to be expounded on, dissected, studied, and committed to memory. It is the essence of who you are. You are a faith being because you were spiritually born of a God of faith.

God has given you the measure of faith. Your regenerated spirit received that measure of faith when you were born again (Romans 12:3). But it gets even better. In Galatians 2:20 Paul says, "I live by the faith of the Son of God." And Ephesians 2:8 says, "By grace are ye saved through faith; and that not of yourselves: it is the gift of God." You were given the same faith Jesus has! God says in 2 Timothy 1:7, "I have not given you the spirit of fear. Wake up! Your spirit is filled with My Spirit and My faith, so your spirit is filled with My love, My power, and the sound mind of Christ."

The Holy Spirit who lives in you is always imparting faith, which is one of the fruits of the Spirit. But there is something more. There is a dynamic, life-altering *spirit of faith* that goes forth and does exploits. The spirit of faith compels you to act, demonstrating the life of God and the devil's defeat in everything you do. So why do so many believers struggle to believe God will do what He says? Why hasn't that spirit of faith taken root in them, developed in their hearts, and manifested in their lives?

The answer lies in recognizing that there is a difference in the *subject* of faith and *the spirit of faith*. Many times ministers treat faith as just another subject to be taught, like end-time prophecy or a marriage seminar. When it is time to teach faith, they pull out their file of notes and teach their people, then put their notes away and don't think about the subject of faith until it's time to teach it again. We should have a steady diet of faith in everything we study because faith comes by hearing God's Word. But just teaching the subject of faith *does not impart the spirit of faith!*

Caught Not Taught

God spoke to me years ago, and said, *"Faith is not merely a subject to be taught; it is a spirit that must be caught."* I'm talking about an attitude, a perspective of faith that flavors and colors every dimension of your life. Because it is impossible to please God without faith (Hebrews 11:6), faith in Him and His Word should be the lens through which you view everything.

Catching the spirit of faith is like catching "school spirit" or "team spirit." A group with school spirit joins together to cheer on the team and encourage one another. They don't just sit and watch. They identify with their team and get involved. They are in the middle of things because their identity and sense of self is wrapped up in being a part of their school.

I live in the state of Alabama, and Alabama is BIG on college football. I mean, these people have an understanding about team spirit and identifying with something bigger than themselves. Even if they never went to college, you would never know it to hear them talk. They can tell you everything about their team, their coach, their game play, everybody their team ever beat, and the score of each game. That's team spirit, and they never even touched a football!

Like someone with school spirit, a believer who has caught the spirit of faith has a heart attitude that is always positive, encouraging, and aggressively pursuing the things of God. The spirit of faith speaks and acts like God and gets the same results. Believers who have caught the spirit of faith identify with their team, and the Captain of their salvation, Jesus. They see themselves as children of the Most High God, operating in His kind of faith (Hebrews 12:9 and Numbers 16:22). They know who their opponent is, what he can and cannot do, and they rehearse their victories over him in Jesus' Name. Faith in God and His Word is the basis of everything they think, say, and do.

The spirit of faith is *caught* by hearing God's Word from others who have it. When you have pastors and teachers who have the spirit of faith, then everything they teach will challenge your faith to step out. Faith is the foundation for every doctrine in the Bible. We are saved by faith. We are justified by faith. We are sanctified by faith. We are forgiven and forgive others by faith. We get wisdom and understanding by faith. We overcome sin by faith. We love ourselves and others by faith. We do everything by faith in God and His Word. And the spirit of faith is not passive. It seeks out and pursues miracles, signs, wonders, and exploits! The spirit of faith dares to believe God in the midst of great odds and impossibilities. Like Abraham, the spirit of faith doesn't consider the circumstances; it only considers what God has said! It goes after God's promise regardless of how it looks or what anyone says.

The spirit of faith is a spirit of victory! It's not something that just sits on a shelf until you have exhausted all your other resources. You've tried everything else and failed miserably, and so you decide you'll get it out, dust if off, and see if it still works. No! Like David when he came against the giant Goliath, the spirit of faith is *looking* for the battle! It is ready to go out and conquer and achieve great things for the Kingdom of God. The spirit of faith always triumphs.

The spirit of faith is not to be treated irreverently; it is much too valuable to the believer. It must be maintained and protected. First of all, we must maintain our relationship with our Heavenly Father. We should be in constant fellowship with Him, communing with the Holy Spirit about every issue of our lives, looking into the Word not only for answers but for revelation and wisdom. We should rehearse His Word, learn it backwards and forwards, so we know our legal standing in every area. We cannot neglect fellowship with God and the life-flow from His Word and maintain the spirit of faith. If we neglect our relationship with Him and His Word, our faith will wither, dry up, and become unproductive in our lives.

We should also associate with those who have the spirit of faith. Early on in my walk with God, I learned that I could receive impartations from great men and women of faith by listening to them teach. I went to their meetings. I would travel to other cities and states and stand in line for hours to get in to hear a faith teacher. I read and reread their books and listened to their tapes constantly. In those early days I worked in construction, and at lunchtime I would go to my truck and listen to tapes. I realized that they were imparting words of life and faith to me, and I valued it more than the food I ate.

Years ago, when I was just learning about the things of God, I had very little contact with any minister other than my local pastor. There was not much teaching of faith available on television, so I depended on the revelation I got from great teachers by listening to them teach the Word of God on cassette tapes.

Just before our daughter was born, I heard Kenneth Copeland on the radio one day, and he said some things that lit a fire in my heart—a fire that's still burning. I ordered his cassette tapes, and we listened to his teaching almost nonstop. We kept the cassette player going all the time, filling our home with the spirit of faith. Our daughter was born during that time, and the Word is all she's ever known. When she began to talk, she would say words like *Mama* and *Daddy,* and then one day when she was about two years old, she walked through the living room and said, "Kenneth Copeland. Fort Worth, Texas, 76112," which were the closing words on all of his tapes! We were exposing our entire family to the spirit of faith and it was taking root in their hearts.

In those days I didn't have personal, face-to-face access to men like Kenneth Copeland or Kenneth Hagin, but I didn't care. What I was interested in was catching the spirit of faith from them and knowing God and His Word in the depth of revelation they were teaching. I developed such a deep respect for them and the message of faith they so faithfully brought to me and my family. And that teaching, and the spirit of faith I caught from them, are greatly responsible for my ministry today. It has brought life and revelation that has affected not only me and my family, but people all around the world!

With modern technology you can view and listen to great ministers of God on radio, television, DVD, CD, cassette tapes, and over the Internet. You can also read their books. These are ways to feed your spirit and keep your faith inspired, encouraged, and strong. But there is nothing better than being in a live meeting, in the presence of the anointing and the spirit of faith, hearing the Word of God taught to you directly and personally. That is the best way to receive and develop the spirit of faith.

Fellowship with the Spirit of Faith

Another important aspect of maintaining the spirit of faith is to fellowship with other believers who have caught it. When I became a Christian I wanted to hang around other Christians all the time. Then after awhile I got to know enough of them to realize there were different kinds of Christians! I began to see that the ones who really took the Word of God seriously and served God with their whole hearts were happier and more productive, and that was the type of believer I wanted to fellowship with.

We should be discerning about those with whom we associate. As Christians, we should spend time with other believers of like precious faith, talking about the things of God. It stirs our faith to rehearse our testimonies of God's faithfulness and listen to others recite their victories. That is part of maintaining the spirit of faith.

It is also very important to guard your heart against those who would try to steal your faith or bring doubt into your thinking. You know who these people are, those who always want to rain on your parade. They have some word of ridicule or rejection, or they mock your faith. Sadly, many times these are people you love, like family members or close friends. But if they continuously come against your faith, you will be better off without them in your daily life. I know there may be times when you have to be around people at work or in family situations, but just guard your heart. If the conversation goes in the wrong direction, redirect it or excuse yourself.

There are believers I shouldn't spend time with unless the Holy Spirit wants me to reach out to them, exhort them, and encourage them to repent and get back on track. My advice to a struggling believer is, "You need to catch the spirit of faith. Hang around this church, hear the Word, listen to the Holy Ghost, and obey the voice of God. Decide today that you're going all the way with God, regardless of what anyone says or whatever happens. The devil and his influences don't have a chance because God is for you. The only thing that will keep you from winning is if you quit."

My words to those believers are spoken to impart an attitude and perspective, which is the spirit of faith. It's God's way of viewing things and doing things. And when they begin to catch that spirit of faith, they will affect everyone else in their lives. Their friends and family may think they're crazy for a while, but when one of them lands in jail or gets a bad report from the doctor, they'll go straight to that crazy Christian who believes God can move mountains and heal the sick!

People want to be around you when they know they can get something from you. That sounds pretty harsh, but think about it a minute. They may make fun of you when they think they have their lives under control and can handle everything themselves, but the minute the devil pulls the rug out from underneath them, they'll only feel safe and find hope from someone they know loves them (even when they called you a fanatic) and has great faith in God.

The spirit of faith is part of your understanding of who you are in Christ, and when you catch it you are compelled by that spirit to possess everything you have in Him. It becomes a driving, motivating force in every action and decision of your life. Don't let the devil use anyone to rob you of your precious faith. I say it this way, "The devil is a liar no matter whose mouth he is using." *Protect the spirit of faith!* Keep (guard) your heart with all diligence for out of it are the issues of life (Proverbs 4:23).

Three Components of a Spirit of Faith

God hath not given us the spirit of fear; but of power, and of love, and of a sound mind.

2 Timothy 1:7

Faith and fear are opposite forces. Faith is the way God does things, and fear is the way the devil does things. In 2 Corinthians 4:13 we read that we have the spirit of faith. Then 2 Timothy 1:7 tells us that the spirit of faith, which is the opposite of fear, consists of power, love, and a sound mind. Let's look at the blessing of each of these components.

Power

The word "power" is a word most Christians are well acquainted with. It is translated from the Greek word *dunamis,* which means "force (literally or figuratively); specially, miraculous power...ability, abundance,...power, strength, violence, mighty (wonderful) work."[1] The English words "dynamo" and "dynamite" are derived from the Greek word *dunamis.*[2] We could say God has not given us the spirit of fear, but He has given us a spirit filled with the explosive, life-changing power of God. This is the power of the Holy Spirit inside us, the same power Jesus was anointed with, walked in, and demonstrated.

In Isaiah 10:27 we read that the yoke of bondage shall be destroyed because of the anointing. The anointing is a tangible empowerment of the Holy Spirit. The Gospels are filled with accounts of how Jesus destroyed yokes of bondage by the anointing of the Holy Spirit. The anointing is the manifested power of God.

> *God anointed Jesus of Nazareth with the Holy Ghost and with power: who went about doing good, and healing all that were oppressed of the devil; for God was with him.*
>
> Acts 10:38

Dunamis is the same power Jesus spoke of to the disciples in Acts 1:4-8. He instructed them to tarry in Jerusalem until they were endued with power. Jesus told them not to leave until they received that explosive, life-changing power of God. He said,

"Don't go anywhere until you get this" because this is the power that raises the dead, heals the sick, and multiplies natural resources. This is the power in which the prophets of old walked and the New Testament saints do mighty exploits. *Dunamis* is part of the spirit of faith.

Why do some believers never experience *dunamis?* God has made it available to all His children, so why are some Christians doing miracles and exploits for God while others have their heads under the covers, afraid to get out of bed in the morning? Again, the Word of God gives us the answer.

> **Be not thou therefore ashamed of the testimony of our Lord,** *nor of me his prisoner; but be thou partaker of the afflictions of the gospel according to the power of God;*
>
> *Who hath saved us, and called us with an holy calling, not according to our works, but according to his own purpose and grace, which was given us in Christ Jesus before the world began,*
>
> *But now is made manifest by the appearing of our Saviour Jesus Christ, who hath abolished death, and hath brought life and immortality to light through the gospel;*
>
> *Whereunto I am appointed a preacher, and an apostle, and a teacher of the Gentiles.*
>
> *For the which cause I also suffer these things: nevertheless **I am not ashamed;** for I know whom I have believed, and am persuaded that he is able to keep that which I have committed unto him against that day.*
>
> 2 Timothy 1:8-12 (emphasis mine)

Twice, once in verse 8 and again in verse 12, Paul tells us not to be ashamed of the Gospel. We are not to be ashamed of the testimony of our Lord and our redemption in Him.

I am not ashamed of the gospel of Christ: for it is the power of God unto salvation to every one that believeth: to the Jew first, and also to the Greek.

For therein is the righteousness of God revealed from faith to faith; as it is written, The just shall live by faith.

Romans 1:16-17

If we want the power of God to be at work in us, we must not be ashamed of the Gospel! Righteousness unto faith is revealed to us when we are not ashamed. When we were born again, we were not ashamed of it. We took it as our own, and it was the power of God to save us. Now that we are saved, we must not be ashamed of any part of the Gospel so that the power of God will work through us to bring others to Christ, to heal the sick, to cast out demons, and to make disciples. These are all works that Jesus commissioned the church to do. Not being ashamed is vital to experiencing the power of God, and the power of God is vital to our completing the work Jesus called us to do.

Paul said he was not ashamed of the Gospel because it is the power of God to *all who believe.* He demonstrated that power again and again. In Acts, chapter 14, Paul passed a lame man who had been crippled from his mother's womb. The man had never walked, but when Paul saw him and perceived that he had faith to be healed, he said to the man, "Stand upright on thy feet," and the man leapt up and walked!

Faith and the power to be healed came to people as Paul preached the Gospel to them. Paul wasn't preaching that healing passed away when Jesus ascended to Heaven. No! We know Paul was preaching with power because it produced faith in the lame man to be healed. He taught that Jesus Christ is "the same, yesterday, and today, and for ever!"

> *Remember them which have the rule over you, who have spoken unto you the word of God: whose faith follow, considering the end of their conversation.*
> *Jesus Christ the same, yesterday, and today, and for ever.*
> *Be not carried about with divers and strange doctrines. For it is a good thing that the heart be established with grace; not with meats, which have not profited them that have been occupied therein.*
>
> Hebrews 13:7-9

Here we are instructed to follow after and submit ourselves to those whose conversation and manner of life we have diligently considered. Listen to them, watch their lives, and determine for ourselves what "the end of their conversation" is. If it is anything other than, "Jesus Christ the same, yesterday, and today, and forever," then we should not follow them. This is part of maintaining and protecting the spirit of faith.

Then in verse 9 Paul instructs us not to be carried about by "strange and diverse doctrines." God is telling us to follow those who preach *Jesus Christ the same*, those who live it and base their lives on that fact. Consider the way they live their lives and what they talk about. If they teach anything other than what Jesus taught and did, it is a strange and diverse doctrine and it will lead us into trouble.

If you want to do the works of Jesus, then you cannot be ashamed of the Gospel. You cannot reduce it to a basic "just make it to Heaven" Gospel. *It is the power of God!* It is the Spirit of God coming to live inside you to completely transform your life. It is Jesus imparting His truth and authority to you so that you can do the works that He did (John 14:12).

Pressure always comes from the enemy, from the world, and from your flesh to try to make you back away from the power of the Gospel. It will come many times from believers who have not studied to show themselves approved of God, rightly dividing the Word of truth (2 Timothy 2:15). This verse in 2 Timothy says that those who do not study and become proficient in the Word of God become ashamed of the Gospel!

When you have caught the spirit of faith, you will sense the Holy Spirit within you empowering you to study, to show yourself approved to God, and to rightly divide His Word. He will bring conviction to your heart if you stray or spend too much time with people or activities that will hinder your walk with Him. He will reveal things to you so that you are not ashamed of the Gospel. He will help you to walk in His power.

God wants you to accomplish His will for your life, and to do that you must have His power! You learn about His power by spending time with Him, getting to know His voice, following His instructions, and obeying His Word. Then, as Hebrews 5:14 teaches, you can have your senses exercised to discern both good and evil, which will cause you to make right choices. You will be alert and guard your heart against any doubt and unbelief that would hinder or stop your faith. Overall, you will walk in His *dunamis* power.

Love

The second component of the spirit of faith is love. We addressed this subject in the first four chapters of this book because Galatians 5:6 says that faith works by love. We learned that love is the foundation of our faith, and that our faith succeeds if it is rooted and grounded in love. Therefore, the spirit of faith produces or works on the basis of love.

It is possible for a person to have faith, but without love their faith produces very little benefit for them. It's like having a car with no tires, set up on blocks. The car is owned by someone but is not functioning as it was designed to function. You cannot say the owner does not have a car, because he does. It just won't take him anywhere. That's what faith is like when you don't operate in God's love. It's like a car on blocks that has no tires. It can't go anywhere. God's love provides the tires that carry your faith and make it productive.

True Bible faith in God will always have God's love as its basis. *Always.* God gave the measure of faith to believers because He loves us. Faith produces in our lives as we return that love to God and show love to others. Faith is activated by love for God and love for others. Love gives and, like all acts of faith, giving must be motivated by love.

The Bible gives particular instructions to husbands about love and giving.

> *Husbands, love your wives, even as Christ also loved the church, and gave himself for it.*
>
> Ephesians 5:25

Some men who are husbands and fathers give to their wives and children only what they are obligated to give. Giving out of obligation and not from a heart of love will always bring heartache. Many have lost their families because they gave only what was required of them or they gave out of necessity rather than love. Wives and children want the love of their husbands and fathers even more than material things. When love is your motive for giving, you give *yourself.* It is not just food and shelter and things you are giving. You are giving security and love.

First Corinthians 13:1-3 says that without love nothing you do in life has any meaning. A man can be a deacon at his church, faithful in serving, even moving in the gifts of the Spirit, but if he does not do all these things from a heart of love, they mean nothing. He can be the greatest provider in the world, but if his motive is anything other than love for his family, willingly giving them his time and affection, he is nothing.

Love is so powerful that people who don't know much about faith and have no clue about resisting the devil or confessing the Word can become very successful just by loving and serving others. The measure of success they achieve can be almost wholly attributed to the fact that they walk in love. Because they are loving, giving people, their prayers avail much and their faith produces.

Walking in love is an awesome thing. There is a freedom and a rest when you walk in love that you can't get any other way. In the midst of storms, whether they are financial, family, health, or any other attack from the enemy, you remain in peace and your faith is strong because you know God loves you and you have such love for others. People who have caught the spirit of faith always walk in love, looking for opportunities to serve and bless others, and doing everything out of love for the Father. Love is a driving, motivating force that compels them to give, to help, to serve, and to be a blessing.

A Sound Mind

The third component of the spirit of faith is a sound mind. This is a mind that is well-balanced, focused correctly, and self-controlled. It has been renewed with the Word of God to the point where even the most volatile emotions come under submission to the Word and the Spirit. People who have caught the spirit of faith are not flaky or weird. They have sound minds, and sound minds produce sound emotions, decisions, and actions.

The greatest tool Satan uses to upset the believer is fear. In chapter 12 we saw the importance of dealing with fear head-on. Allowing just one fearful thought can throw you off balance, cause you to lose focus, and send you on the road to destruction.

According to 2 Timothy 1:7, fear is a spirit. There is an entity known as the spirit of fear, and the devil is the chief spirit behind it. However, just because you feel afraid does not mean you are possessed by a demon of fear. Everyone feels fear from time to time, and everyone has to deal with individual fears. That doesn't mean they are demon possessed. They may believe the thoughts and lies that come to them and become oppressed and fearful, but they are not possessed by the spirit of fear.

Some people are predisposed to fear. They carry a nervous attitude and react to the smallest thing that startles them. Any little sound will make them jump. But no matter how fearful they are, Jesus came to deliver them of all fear, anxiety, and nervousness. He delivers them by saving them, filling them with His love, and giving them His Word that frees them from the bondage of fear. First John 4:18 puts it this way, "There is no fear in love; but perfect love casteth out fear: because fear hath torment. He that feareth is not made perfect in love."

Believers who are still fighting fear must pursue being established in God's love and being renewed in the spirit of their minds. That means to have their minds, attitudes, and emotions ruled by the Word of God. Believers should respond to every natural attack or circumstance by a mind trained and disciplined by the Word of God. Every obstacle, every uncertainty, and every crisis should be met with the response, "Glory to God! God loves me and this is another opportunity for God to show Himself strong and demonstrate His love!" We know that no matter what happens, in the end, we win!

Your sound, renewed mind thinks and responds like God when you are full of His Word.

> *As it is written, Eye hath not seen, nor ear heard, neither have entered into the heart of man, the things which God hath prepared for them that love him.*
> *But God hath revealed them unto us by his Spirit; for the Spirit searcheth all things, yea, the deep things of God.*
> *For what man knoweth the things of man, save the spirit of man which is in him; even so the things of God knoweth no man, but the Spirit of God.*
> *Now we have received, not the spirit of the world, but the spirit which is of God; that we might know the things that are freely given to us of God.*
>
> 1 Corinthians 2:9-12

In verse 12 Paul says we have not received the *spirit* of the world, but the *spirit* which is of God. He goes on to say that we should know the things God has freely given us. By inspiration of the Holy Ghost, Paul is making a contrast between the way the world thinks and lives and the way the Christian thinks and lives.

We have sound minds because we have our minds renewed to God's Word and all that He has provided. We are not led by what we see or feel. People in the world, on the other hand, rely entirely on their own abilities and strength. "What they see is what they get." They are limited to their five senses and carnal thinking. They are not spiritually alive to God, drawing on His wisdom and ability.

> *Which things also we speak, not in the words which man's wisdom teacheth, but which the Holy Ghost teacheth; comparing spiritual things with spiritual.*
>
> *But the natural man receiveth not the things of the Spirit of God: for they are foolishness unto him: neither can he know them, because they are spiritually discerned.*
>
> *But he that is spiritual judgeth all things, yet he himself is judged of no man.*
>
> *For who hath known the mind of the Lord, that he may instruct him? But we have the mind of Christ.*
>
> 1 Corinthians 2:13-16

The latter part of verse 16 says that "we have the mind of Christ." *Goodspeed's New Testament* says, "We share the thoughts of Christ."[3] Sharing the thoughts of Christ is how a sound mind works. People who have the mind of Christ don't respond like the world responds. They respond like Jesus responds, with the Word of God.

Most people are familiar with Pavlov's experiments with dogs. He trained them to believe that when a bell rang, they would be fed. The sound of a bell meant mealtime, and their senses and bodies reacted to what they believed. They began to salivate and anticipate food, and even their involuntary instincts responded to the external stimulus of a ringing bell.

People have been trained in the same way. Some have been trained to think that if something bad *can* happen, it *will* happen. Murphy's Law is the law they live by: "If anything can go wrong it will go wrong." You may even hear them say, "I knew that was going to happen; it was just bound to." That kind of talking opens the door to bad things and even binds it to them, ordaining it to come to pass.

I was in a man's office one day when his phone rang. He answered it, and the first words out of his mouth were, "Oh, no." His face looked sadder and sadder. When he hung up the phone, he said, "Every phone call I've had today has been bad news. My wife called to say the water heater blew up, then the next call was that the car had broken down. I don't even want to answer the phone again to find out what else has happened."

In one day's time that man had been trained to think that the phone ringing meant bad news. The devil was having a field day with him. He was thinking like the world, expecting the worst. It reminded me of that song, "Gloom, Despair, and Agony on Me," written and sung by Buck Owens and Roy Clark on the television show *Hee-Haw!*

A sound mind knows that good news comes by way of telephone just as easily as bad news. I go to my mailbox expecting good things. When my phone rings, I expect good news. And when bad news does come, a sound mind responds with faith in God and His Word instead of despairing.

I want to warn you that living like this doesn't always win you a popularity contest! When we think and react by the Word of God, the world thinks we are crazy. People say we have lost all reason. This even happened to the Apostle Paul.

As he thus spake for himself, Festus said with a loud voice, Paul, thou art beside thyself, much learning doth make thee mad.
But he said, I am not mad, most noble Festus; but speak forth the words of truth and soberness.

Acts 26:24-25

Festus worshipped Nero, who was the Caesar in that day. Paul worshipped the Lord Jesus Christ. When Paul told Festus about Jesus, Festus said Paul was beside himself and had gone mad. This is how opposite the world's thinking is to the way God thinks. Unbelievers often view a sound mind as being mad!

The world, and many times well-meaning Christians, may think you have lost your mind when you begin to think and speak and act with a sound mind. Your own family may call you a fanatic and say that this "faith stuff" has made you go off the deep end. People didn't care when you lived a wild life, told dirty jokes, and drank too much; but now that you are thinking and talking like God, they treat you like you are crazy!

If you have ever stepped out in faith in front of people who are not saved, you have faced persecution. The spirit of the world cannot understand and even hates the spirit of faith. You can also face persecution from other believers who haven't caught the spirit of faith. They don't understand what you are saying or why you are doing what you are doing. That is because the mind of Christ, a sound mind, sees everything through the eyes of faith in God and His Word. You see the answer in your spirit, but they see only the problem in the natural. Things of the spirit can't be seen with the natural eye or heard with the natural ear. They must be seen through the eye of faith and heard by ears attuned to the Word of God.

My thoughts are not your thoughts, neither are your ways my ways, saith the LORD. For as the heavens are higher than the earth, so are my ways higher that your ways, and my thoughts than your thoughts.

Isaiah 55:8-9

This is the spirit of faith: thinking, speaking, and acting like God. God's plan for His children is simple. When you think like God thinks, talk like God talks, and act like God acts; you will live like God lives!

CHAPTER 14

Developing the Spirit of Faith

The issue of faith in God is of primary importance. In 2 Corinthians 13:5 we are instructed to examine ourselves to see whether we are in faith. Hebrews 10:38 says, "The just shall live by faith," and Hebrews 11:6 says, "without faith it is impossible to please God." No other Bible subject is put in that category. The Bible doesn't say, "Without good works it's impossible to please God." We can readily see that the issue of faith in God and His Word is essential to the believer.

Everybody operates in faith or by faith from time to time. Even unbelievers operate in faith. They believe things will happen, good things or bad things. That's just the way people are because that's the way God made human beings to function. As believers, we operate in faith in God and His Word. Our faith is rooted and grounded in the love of the Creator of all things, and our faith is based on His Word.

We are saved by faith. We believed that a sinless Man we had never seen, who lived two thousand years ago, shed His blood and died for our sins by beatings and crucifixion; and three days later He was resurrected. We believe He did all this to pay our debt for sin and reconcile us to God. Then we completely surrendered our lives to this Man. We didn't see Him do any of the miracles the Bible reports He did. We didn't watch as He was crucified. Personally, He has never appeared to me in the flesh since He was resurrected. And yet, I have made Him the Lord of my life. That is the God kind of faith in action, and every believer has experienced it. The natural mind cannot comprehend this kind of faith because it is the God kind of faith, and it is spiritual because He the Father of spirits (Hebrews 12:9).

Now that we are saved and have this great God kind of faith in our spirits, we must develop it and operate effectively in it. I'm going to share four things that will help you to walk successfully in faith.

1. Have the Bible Attitude Concerning Affliction

We having the same spirit of faith, according as it is written, I believed, and therefore have I spoken; we also believe, and therefore speak;
Knowing that he which raised up the Lord Jesus shall raise up us also by Jesus, and shall present us with you.

For all things are for your sakes, that the abundant grace might
through the thanksgiving of many redound to the glory of God.
For which cause we faint not; but though our outward man perish,
yet the inward man is renewed day by day.
For our light affliction, which is but for a moment, worketh for us
a far more exceeding and eternal weight of glory;
While we look not at the things which are seen, but at the things
which are not seen: for the things which are seen are temporal; but
the things which are not seen are eternal.

2 Corinthians 4:13-18

In verse 13, Paul says that we have the same spirit of faith. Then he goes into an explanation of some of the characteristics of this spirit of faith. Our spirits believe and speak, knowing God is faithful to perform His Word. We do all things with a heart of thanksgiving, which gives God glory. The spirit of faith does not faint when the going gets tough because our inward man gets stronger and stronger as we walk in faith.

Then Paul deals with affliction, and his attitude toward affliction is entirely different than that of most people, including most Christians. By afflictions, he is referring to tests, trials, difficulties, obstacles in our way, and all the pressures we face in our Christian life. In 2 Corinthians, chapter 11, Paul gives a list of the "light afflictions" he endured.

Are they ministers of Christ? (I speak as a fool) I am more; in
labours more abundant, in stripes above measure, in prisons more
frequent, in deaths oft.
Of the Jews five times received I forty stripes save one.

Thrice was I beaten with rods, once was I stoned, thrice I suffered shipwreck, a night and a day I have been in the deep;

In journeyings often, in perils of waters, in perils of robbers, in perils by mine own countrymen, in perils by the heathen, in perils in the city, in perils in the wilderness, in perils in the sea, in perils among false brethren;

In weariness and painfulness, in watchings often, in hunger and thirst, in fastings often, in cold and nakedness.

Beside those things that are without, that which cometh upon me daily, the care of all the churches.

Verses 23-28

Paul dealt with horrible things. He was beaten, imprisoned, robbed, left for dead, stoned, shipwrecked, in hunger and thirst, and in nakedness. How could Paul call these afflictions *light?*

This is another spiritual concept that the natural mind and the world cannot understand. How could anyone possibly view physical torture and persecution, catastrophe, perils of all kinds, hunger and lack, and almost overwhelming responsibility as "light affliction?" Paul could because he had developed the spirit of faith.

Every human being faces the storms of life and encounters problems, and believers are no exception to this. However, the way believers should look at them and deal with them is totally different from someone who doesn't know God and His love and goodness. We have His authority, wisdom, and strength to make every stumbling block a stepping-stone to greater happiness and success. We magnify Him in the face of adversity until that adversity looks tiny and helpless in the face of His power. We have the attitude that each affliction is another opportunity for God to show Himself strong in our behalf, for miracles to take place, and for all those around us to see His goodness— which leads to repentance and salvation.

I made up my mind years ago that I would have the spirit of faith and would live according to faith no matter what happened to me or anyone around me. I have taken the attitude that I will never lose. I *cannot* lose. For me to fail, God would have to fail, and God is not going to fail! I know that as long as I am hooked up to God, as long as I am standing on His Word and walking in His love, I'm going to make it. I am going over and not under, regardless of what I face.

As for you, be calm and cool and steady, accept and suffer unflinchingly every hardship, do the work of an evangelist, fully perform all the duties of your ministry.

2 Timothy 4:5 AMP

Paul used the phrase, "suffer unflinchingly every hardship." This is the attitude of the believer who has caught the spirit of faith. This phrase reminds me of when I was a kid in school. Some of the boys would gather on the playground or the football field to see who was the strongest and toughest. Often it would come down to a contest of swapping licks. You would tighten your arm or shoulder muscles, or wherever you had agreed to receive the blow. (We always did it on the shoulder.)

The other guy would rear back, ball up his fist, and hit you as hard as he could. Then it was your turn, and you could hit him back just as hard as you could. The first one to flinch lost the contest. The last one standing was the best man.

Paul is not saying you should put on a mask or a false front, being too proud to tell anyone you are in pain or in need of help. Nor is he telling you to be ashamed if anybody knows you're going through a rough time. He's saying that when the devil takes his best shot, don't flinch or complain. Instead, hold on to the big picture, knowing this affliction is light, it will pass, and you will come out victorious. All the enemy knows then is that he has dealt you his best shot and couldn't stop you. Then you open your mouth and blow him away with the Word of God!

The spirit of faith remains calm, cool, and steady; enduring unflinchingly every hardship. Not flinching means not complaining, blaming, or magnifying the devil's power. Not flinching means staying steady because you have caught the spirit of faith and know that in Jesus you have His superior power, His unconditional love, and a sound mind. The only way the devil can beat you is if you quit.

The devil is never going to make me flinch. I already know he is going to do his best to find an open door, any cracked window, or a hole in the ceiling to try to come in and destroy me. That's his mission. He can take his best shot, but I've learned that greater is He that is in me than he that is in the world (1 John 4:4). When it comes to affliction, the spirit of faith always takes the attitude that it's light and it will pass.

For years I have noticed many teachers and believers sidestep any discussion of affliction. Then, at the first sign of trouble or perhaps if trouble persists beyond what they expected, they fold because they haven't settled it in their hearts that it is light and it will pass. Usually, when the Bible mentions affliction, it is referring to dealing with persecution for your faith, anguish because you have been hurt or disappointed, or suffering things we've brought on ourselves by bad choices, selfishness, or yielding to the flesh.

There's nothing worse than finding ourselves in a mess, usually of our own making, and having to face our flesh and all our character flaws. The Holy Ghost will shine the light on these areas of weakness, temptation, and stinkin' thinkin', and we just ignore Him until those very things get us into such trouble that the only way out is to deal with our flesh and our behavior.

The truth is, most of the time we are afflicted because the devil has taken advantage of a situation we provided for him. The things we run from or refuse to deal with are the very things that Satan will use to defeat us. That's why it is important to face these things when the Holy Ghost taps us on the shoulder and says, "It's time to deal with this."

Thou therefore endure hardness, as a good soldier of Jesus Christ.
2 Timothy 2:3

Enduring hardness as a good soldier of Jesus Christ doesn't mean we reconcile ourselves to a life of drudgery, pain, suffering, and unpleasantness. It simply means we settle it in our own hearts and minds ahead of time that our attitude toward any affliction that comes our way will be that it is *light*. Light and easy. It's going to be easy to overcome because we are in Christ Jesus. It's also going to be temporary. It will last a limited amount of time at best. Every war in history had a beginning and an end.

When we view our afflictions as light, the devil cannot discourage us or stop us from growing up and moving forward in God. Having the right attitude toward affliction is essential to maintaining a powerful walk of faith.

2. *Focus on the Vision God Has Given You*

Our light affliction, which is but for a moment, worketh for us a far more exceeding and eternal weight of glory;
While we look not at the things which are seen, but at the things which are not seen: for the things which are seen are temporal; but the things which are not seen are eternal.

2 Corinthians 4:17-18

Verse 17 says that our light affliction, which lasts only a short time, works for us. And what it works is so much greater than we can imagine because it brings eternal glory to our lives. In order to have that eternal glory working for us, the Holy

Spirit tells us to look at something. He tells us to look at the things which are not seen, those things that are eternal. Our light affliction works to produce an eternal weight of glory only when we look at the eternal things that are not seen.

> The light of the body is the eye: if therefore thine eye be single, thy whole body shall be full of light.
> But if thine eye be evil, thy whole body shall be full of darkness. If therefore the light that is in thee be darkness, how great is that darkness!
>
> Matthew 6:22-23

Jesus tells us in verse 22 that your eye, what you are focusing on, determines how much light you will walk in. If you concentrate on problems and difficulties, then your light is dim and little or no light or illumination is available to show you the way out. But if you concentrate on the faithfulness and greatness of God, His Word will be a light to your path. He will show you the way of escape. And you'll be lit up from the inside out.

Again and again I've seen the difference living for God can make in a person's life. I've seen sinners, who are lost, undone, and on their way to hell. Their countenance is dark. Even their skin seems dull and lifeless. Then they accept Jesus as Lord, and the next thing you know, light is radiating out of their eyes. Life has come and God's glory is all over them.

The same thing happens to believers who backslide and, after serving the flesh for a season, repent and come back to

God. One day a young man came into my office crying for help. He had been into drugs on and off for many years and was hooked on crack cocaine. He was a Christian, but he had degenerated into the depths of addiction and was desperate. He had lost his job, lost his health, and he came to me as a last resort. He said, "If I can't get some help here, there's nowhere to go. I'll just kill myself."

I counseled him and dealt with that spirit of suicide, then I talked to him about getting into a Christian rehabilitation and residency program that would get him away from all the temptations and carnal influences he was around every day. He agreed to commit himself to a year-long program.

A couple of weeks later I was in that area of the state to do some meetings, and I arrived at the church a little late. As I was being ushered to my seat, I felt a tap on my shoulder. I turned around and there was the young man who had come to me for help. He reached out and grabbed me in a bear hug. The transformation in him was so remarkable that I didn't recognize him! After the hug I backed up, looked at his smiling face, and thought, *My goodness. That's the fellow that was in my office a few weeks ago!* He just glowed with the glory of God.

That's the way God wants all of us to look, radiating His glory and happiness. But that will happen only if we focus our attention on the big picture—God's plan and purpose for our lives.

Eternal Purpose

God hasn't called all of us to be in full-time pulpit ministry. However, we are all called to have a part of the great harvest of souls. He wants us corporately to evangelize the world and to be a blessing to others. You may not be called to fill a pulpit and preach or go door to door and witness, but wherever you are, you can tell people about Jesus.

The Bible says we all have been given the ministry of reconciliation (2 Corinthians 5:18), and the important thing is that you are willing to do your part. You may be called to support outreach and missions ministries financially if you aren't directly involved. And if you are in business or another profession where you have continual contact with people in the world, God has given you your own mission field! Wherever you are called, being a part of what God is doing is what is going to light you up.

When you are lit by a passion to serve God, you give warmth and illumination to others. In John, chapter 4, we read the story of Jesus meeting the woman at the well. Because we know that Jesus is the Son of God, the sinless Lamb of God sent from Heaven to be our Savior, we sometimes forget that He was human, just like we are. Although He never sinned, when He was on the earth, He was tempted in all ways like we are. His body got tired and weary, and He got hungry and suffered thirst.

Then cometh he to a city of Samaria, which is called Sychar, near to the parcel of ground that Jacob gave to his son Joseph.

Now Jacob's well was there. Jesus therefore, being wearied with his journey, sat thus on the well: and it was about the sixth hour.

There cometh a woman of Samaria to draw water: Jesus saith unto her, Give me to drink.

John 4:5-7

Jesus had a physical body like ours, and He sat down on this well because He was tired, thirsty, and hungry. He had sent the disciples into the city to buy meat, and while they were gone, He met this woman at the well and told her about the living water that satisfies forever.

Jesus...said unto her, Whosoever drinketh of this water shall thirst again:

But whosoever drinketh of the water that I shall give him shall never thirst; but the water that I shall give him shall be in him a well of water springing up into everlasting life.

John 4:13-14

Jesus talked briefly to the woman at the well, and then the Holy Spirit gave Jesus a word of knowledge about her. He told her that she was not married and was living in sin with a man. In verse 19 she said, "Sir, I perceive that thou art a prophet," and by the end of their discussion she also saw that Jesus was the Messiah. She immediately went into the city and told the people about Him.

In the mean while his disciples prayed him, saying, Master, eat.

But he said unto them, I have meat to eat that ye know not of.

Therefore said the disciples one to another, Hath any man brought him aught to eat?

Jesus saith unto them, My meat is to do the will of him that sent me, and to finish his work.

Say not ye, There are yet four months, and then cometh harvest? behold, I say unto you, Lift up your eyes, and look on the fields; for they are white already to harvest.

John 4:31-35

Jesus had come to the well tired, thirsty, and hungry, but as He began to minister to the woman He was inspired and strengthened. Doing what God called Him to do quickened and brought strength to His mortal body. When His disciples tried to get Him to eat natural food, He said, "No, I have meat to eat you don't understand." Doing the will of God strengthened Jesus spiritually just as natural food strengthens the body.

Then Jesus said, "Lift up your eyes!"

When God tells someone to lift up their eyes, it is to get their eyes off their temporary circumstances and back on what is eternally important. In Genesis 13:14, God said to Abram, "Lift up your eyes and look at all the land I'm going to give you." He put Abram's focus back on the vision and promise for his life. God wants us to lift up our eyes and get a fresh vision of our lives every day. Whenever we are weary, discouraged, and feel like the whole world is against us, we simply have to lift up our eyes and see our eternal purpose to be refreshed and recharged. Our eternal purpose is doing our part to bring in His harvest of souls.

Faith Has Vision

The single most defining characteristic of the spirit of faith is *vision*. Vision is supernatural insight from God to your spirit that reveals His plan and purpose for your life. Your eyes are opened, and you can see yourself doing what God has destined you to do. That vision becomes the motivating force that drives you toward your goal, relentlessly pursuing the fulfillment of all God has put in your heart to do. Vision is determined to see God's will come to pass and is unwilling to give up or be denied.

God gives every born-again believer a vision for their life. We each have a part to play in His plan for mankind. First Corinthians 12:14-26 says that each member of the body of Christ is unique, beloved of God, and vital. If you don't know what your place is yet, the Lord is saying to you, "Lift up your eyes! Find your place in the body of Christ and go forward with a renewed spirit, with renewed vision."

What has this got to do with faith? Without vision, faith has nothing to do! When you catch the spirit of faith, God has something for you to do and He will reveal that to you. And when you stay focused on your purpose, you are continually inspired and motivated. People with vision are people who are filled with the life of God. They have His energy and His passion to see the work completed. They are going places!

Vision is the "meat from Heaven" Jesus tried to get the disciples to see. Meat gives the physical body energy and strength, and our spiritual meat is the vision God gives us. Vision reveals our purpose and our part in the plan of God, and following after and doing His will gives us joy and renewed strength.

I like a good hamburger, but the energy it gives me soon runs out. I need to eat meat every day to keep my energy up and nourish my body. The same is true spiritually. Every day I need to renew my vision, get energized and refreshed by focusing on what God has called me to do that day and in the future.

If you wake up every morning with this focus, your heart will be continually filled with faith and joy.

3. Don't Get Entangled

No man that warreth entangleth himself with the affairs of this life; that he may please him who hath chosen him to be a soldier.
2 Timothy 2:4

When you get entangled in the affairs of life, you forget that you are an eternal being. Everything you experience in life, pleasant and unpleasant, will pass. You can get as entangled in the good things as the bad things and forget the big picture God has put in your heart. When that happens and you become wrapped up in your everyday responsibilities, forgetting your eternal perspective and purpose, you also can fall into the habits of thinking and speaking like the world. Eventually the Word of God fades from view, you revert to your old ways of thinking and talking, and your faith becomes lifeless.

Don't fight in the flesh. Don't gossip. Don't compare yourself with others. Don't be driven to compete in the sense that you have to be better than somebody or to do something bigger or better than they do it. You must not do things the way the world does them or think the way the world thinks. If you are entangled in offenses, hurt feelings, frustrations, and resentment, it's hard to believe that God will bless you. However, when you are free of these entanglements, your faith is also free to pursue your calling and all the blessings of God. Because faith works by love and faith without works is dead, we must do the works of love to have powerful faith that pleases God.

Ephesians 5:1 NASB says we are to imitate God, and He is a God of faith and love. When we refuse to be tangled up in the ways and thinking of the world and instead walk in faith and love, we are walking like God walks.

Start imitating God by speaking words of kindness and goodness to those around you, by forgiving them and being patient, not holding offenses against them, and not being mean-spirited when they do you wrong. Romans 12:21 says, "Be not overcome of evil, but overcome evil with good." God overcomes evil by pouring in goodness. He overcame sin and death by sending Jesus to die for mankind's sin, which was the ultimate act of love. That's why Romans 2:4 says that it is the goodness of God that leads people to repentance. When they encounter the awesome love of God in the sacrifice of Jesus, they cannot resist His love and are convicted of their sin. They compare their weakness and inability with His goodness and love, then they gladly receive Him as Lord and Savior and are born again.

No matter what you do or what profession you may be in, you can walk in faith and love and make an impact on those around you. One of the dearest friends I have is a businessman, and I love his business attitude. When it comes to his competitors, he says, "You know, there's plenty of business out there for all of us. I just pray blessings on every one of them. I'm not going to try to defeat anybody or force anyone out of business. I'm simply going to do what God has given me to do."

This man is so refreshing to be around because he has vision for what the Lord has called him to do, and he's not threatened by anyone else with a similar vision. He's walking in faith and love like his Heavenly Father. But all too often I see Christians trying to compete and prosper using the world's ways and ideas. They get entangled in natural circumstances and let personalities and the actions and attitudes of others hinder their faith in God. They have forgotten that the battle is the Lord's and the weapons of our warfare are not of the natural realm (1 Samuel 17:47 and 2 Corinthians 10:4). Many have forgotten to put on the armor of God and are losing because they are trying to fight a natural battle.

> *Finally, my brethren, be strong in the Lord, and in the power of his might.*
>
> *Put on the whole armour of God, that ye may be able to stand against the wiles of the devil.*
>
> *For we wrestle not against flesh and blood, but against principalities, against powers, against the rulers of the darkness of this world, against spiritual wickedness in high places.*
>
> Ephesians 6:10-12

Our battles in this life are not with flesh and blood. People are not our enemies. Our enemies are the devil and his demons that influence, manipulate, and control people. Since we are not in a natural flesh and blood battle, we don't use natural weapons. Our weapons are not carnal, but are mighty through God, pulling down strongholds (2 Corinthians 10:4)! Our weapons are our faith, our authority in the Name of Jesus, and our ability to speak God's Word. When we activate our faith and speak the Word of God, we wield the sword of the Spirit and we cannot fail!

> *They that are after the flesh do mind the things of the flesh; but they that are after the Spirit the things of the Spirit.*
>
> *For to be carnally minded is death; but to be spiritually minded is life and peace.*
>
> Romans 8:5-6

Carnal people set their minds on the things of the flesh and are dead to the things of God. The story of the prodigal son in Luke, chapter 15, tells us that this young man took his inheritance, left his father's house, and went out to enjoy the world and to do things his own way. He ended up broke, eating with pigs in a pigsty. Realizing that even his father's servants had a better life than he was living, he finally went home. His father rejoiced when he returned, saying "My son was dead, and is alive again," (Luke 15:24).

As a believer, when you become entangled in the things of this world, you look spiritually dead. The Apostle Paul had a word for Christians who got caught up in the world.

> *Wherefore he saith, Awake thou that sleepest, and arise from the dead, and Christ shall give thee light.*
>
> Ephesians 5:14

Paul says, "You believers who are out in the world and are asleep among the spiritually dead, wake up! Get out of there, and Christ will fill you with His life and light."

There are too many Christians who look unsaved and act unsaved because they are living carnal lives instead of following after the Word and the Spirit. They are almost dead to the things of God because they choose to live in a pigsty, eating hog food instead of living for God and eating at the Master's table. Then they wonder why their faith is so weak.

Hog food can be served in many different forms. It can be gossip. It can be vengeance. It can be unforgiveness. It can be just plain carnal, worldly talk of doubt and unbelief. That is not the kind of food God intended for His children to consume. Wrong words, actions, and attitudes will starve your faith in God and His Word because you were not designed to partake of it. And it will get you into a flesh and blood battle. You will fight your battles in your human understanding, reasoning, and strength. Even if you win a battle, you will be so weak and worn out, you won't be able to enjoy the victory!

Although we are *in* the world, we are not *of* the world. We are born of God, and we "live by the faith of the Son of God" (Galatians 2:20). When we live our lives by the faith of the Son of God, we walk in greater blessing and know the peace that passes all understanding. God provided it for us and it is ours to enjoy—and to keep us from being entangled with the affairs of this life.

4. Maintain an Attitude of Faith

The spirit of faith is an aggressive faith. When you have caught the spirit of faith, you begin to act like Jesus. Your decisions and actions are determined by the Word of God, and it influences everything you think and say. You live to please Jesus and want others to see Jesus in you, bringing glory to Him. Living by "the faith of the Son of God" is a perspective and way of life that keeps you rooted and grounded in love, passionate about God's Word, and determined to follow the Holy Spirit.

Those who catch the spirit of faith are the devil's worst nightmare.

The spirit of faith scares the devil because he knows that his destructive maneuvers in the life of a believer are going to be exposed, attacked, and defeated. The spirit of faith does not retreat when under attack; it responds immediately with the Word of God. The spirit of faith takes on challenges no one else will consider. It adopts an attitude that says, "God has called us to do this, and we're going to do it. We're going to build a church to preach the Gospel and bring in the harvest of souls. We're going to make disciples and train up leaders in places where no one knows Jesus and everyone is hostile to us. We're going to do what God has called us to do, knowing He will take care of us and supply everything we need."

Satan is not afraid of our pretty buildings and all the improvements we make to them. He's not afraid of our fellowships and organizations. But he cowers in fright when we rise up in the spirit of faith, believing and trusting God and His Word, and go out and do the works of Jesus. He's shaking in his shoes when we use our authority and rule over him by the power of God. The spirit of faith terrifies the devil because the only way he can control the earth is to control people, and he loses his influence and control over people when they learn who they are in Christ Jesus. He can't dominate or oppress those who exercise their authority over him and walk in the spirit of faith.

The spirit of faith is also a spirit of excellence. There is no mediocrity in the faith of the Son of God. Unfortunately, we see too many Christians who settle for less than God's best for their lives. But the spirit of faith will never settle for less than what God has provided. It's like the bold faith of Shadrach, Meshach, and Abednego, who went into the fiery furnace rather than bow to anyone but God. They came out of the fire unscathed, without even the smell of smoke!

> *The princes, governors, and captains, and the king's counsellors, being gathered together, saw these men, upon whose bodies the fire had no power, nor was an hair of their head singed, neither were their coats changed, nor the smell of fire had passed on them.*
>
> Daniel 3:27

Too many Christians are satisfied to come out of a fiery trial just barely alive. They don't care if they smell like smoke. They don't even care if their hair and clothes are half burned off. They're just grateful to have made it out of the fire. Those who have caught the spirit of faith are not satisfied with that! They don't want to wade through the water; they want to walk on top of it! They don't want to waste their time and energy climbing mountains Jesus said would be removed when they speak to them (Matthew 17:20). And when the devil shows up, they don't run away from him; they run toward him! They know that

God and His Word are for them, so who can be against them and prevail? Not the devil and not anyone he influences!

Too often God's children live beneath His gracious and generous provision. It reminds me of an incident that took place several years ago with a young man who was a member of our church. This young man had leased a nice apartment in town, and one day he called me and said, "Pastor, God has blessed me."

"That's great! What has He done?" I asked.

"You know how much I like to watch sports. Well, in my new place, my television will pick up ESPN!"

"Good for you" I said, wondering what the big deal was.

He said, 'No, you don't understand. I don't have cable. It's picking ESPN up on the rabbit ears!"

I said, "It is?"

He said, "Yeah, it comes in kind of fuzzy. You have to strain to watch it, but you can see it. And I got to watch the playoffs the other night!" He was so excited about getting a fuzzy ESPN picture.

About a month later I saw him and asked, "How's your television doing? Are you still getting ESPN?"

He shook his head with a funny look on his face and said, "Yeah, I didn't know it, but when I leased that apartment, cable service was included with it. I had the television against the wall near the cable connection, so the rabbit ears were picking up the signal off the cable wire. When I found out that cable service was provided, I connected it to my TV, and now the picture comes in perfectly clear."

The Lord said to me, "That's the picture of too many of My children. They are content with so little and don't know how much I want to bless them. They are picking up a fuzzy picture thinking there's only so much the faith I gave them can do. But Jesus purchased the whole package, and all they have to do is just plug in to Me and receive all I've purchased for them."

Isn't that the truth? How many of us have made the mistake of settling for what the devil, our natural thinking, or other people said we had to settle for. God wants us to catch the spirit of faith, believe what His Word says, and act like it is true. Jesus Christ has redeemed us from the curse of the law, and we can walk in our redemptive rights and privileges twenty-four hours a day. We don't have to settle for fuzzy pictures! We can see it like God meant us to see it.

As you live a consistent life of faith, counting every affliction as light, keeping your eyes on your eternal purpose, and refusing to be entangled in the everyday affairs of this life, you will have a powerful impact on all those around you. You will not only enjoy the victories and the blessings of God, you will change the lives of those you touch.

CHAPTER 15

Faith That Pleases God

Faith is not something that God looks at apart from everything else. It is an attribute and characteristic of God. Faith is the way and the means He uses to create and to do everything. When He gives us His faith at the new birth, we have fellowship with Him and begin to live by faith.

As I've traveled the world, I have seen a lot of people—and many of them are Christians—who are totally ignorant about what pleases God and how He wants them to live their lives. They don't know Him because they either don't know His Word or have been wrongly taught. Therefore, they don't know His love because you have to know God in order to know His love. Because faith works by love and they don't understand or experience God's love, then their faith in Him is distorted. They believe that they must prove themselves to God and suffer great pain in order to please Him or to get Him to respond to them.

In 1988 my wife and I went to Spain with another couple in ministry to spy out the land. We had a desire to go and see what was happening spiritually and make some contacts. In one place we visited the showpiece of the city, which is a beautiful, massive, old cathedral. It probably covered two city blocks, and the main sanctuary was so large that they were holding six different masses in it at the same time.

As we walked up to the front doors, we noticed a man who was on his knees, arms spread out on either side, head down, not moving a muscle. After spending some time walking around inside the cathedral, we went outside to find the man still in front of the doors in the same position. We realized he may have been there for hours or was intending to be there for hours. He was doing penance, thinking that by staying there in the hot sun until his knees were bleeding and his body was sunburned and dehydrated, God would see fit to forgive him. Or maybe he had a personal need or affliction, and he was offering himself as a sacrifice so that God would hear his prayers and help him.

As I walked past him, I couldn't help but think, *There's a man who doesn't know God. Bless his heart.* He thought he was doing something that would please God or get His attention, thus putting him in position to receive something he needed from God.

If that man knew God and His Word, He would know that God had already been satisfied with the perfect sacrifice of

Jesus. When Jesus gave His life as sacrifice for all our sin, he paid our debt in full and we were forgiven and healed in full. Our redemption was complete—spirit, soul, and body.

That man may have been born again, but he did not know God or understand and experience His love and grace. Therefore, he didn't know how to walk in "the faith of the Son of God," which is what pleases Him.

That man's actions demonstrated the dilemma of trying to please God but being ignorant of the benefits and privileges of his salvation, not knowing God and His love for him. But sometimes believers fall prey to another type of error. These are those who know God and have experienced His love, and they use their faith and God honors it. God will move in power and use them to lead people to Jesus, heal the sick, cast out demons, feed the poor, and do other works by His Spirit. But if that believer does not continue to get to know God and do these things by His love, they are eventually going to hit a wall, and much of what they have accomplished will crumble. We know this from 1 Corinthians 13:1-3, which says that we can do many great things in the Name of Jesus, but it means nothing if we don't do it in love. Acts of faith receive God's seal of approval only when they are motivated by love.

The fact that people were saved and healed and filled with the Holy Ghost doesn't change just because the motive of the individual who ministered to them was something other than love. However, sooner or later that minister will come to a crossroads in their walk of faith by love. They will have a choice set before them, and the choice they make will determine their future walk with God and His ability to bless them and use them in His Kingdom. If they step out of love to follow the lust of their flesh, financial gain, or pride in being well-known or famous, their days of usefulness to God are numbered.

Faith and Love Are Behaviors

Love is patient, love is kind and is not jealous; love does not brag and is not arrogant,

does not act unbecomingly; it does not seek its own, is not provoked, does not take into account a wrong suffered,

does not rejoice in unrighteousness, but rejoices with the truth;

bears all things, believes all things, hopes all things, endures all things.

Love never fails; but if there are gifts of prophecy, they will be done away; if there are tongues, they will cease; if there is knowledge, it will be done away.

1 Corinthians 13:4-8 NASB

We are born of God and He is love, so we know that our nature is love. Consequently, our behavior should reflect who we are in Him. In verse 5, love does not behave itself unbecomingly, so it must behave in another way. There are specific ways love behaves, and the Bible says that there is one behavior that demonstrates the greatest love of all.

Greater love hath no man than this, that a man lay down his life for his friends.

John 15:13

Laying down your life can be as simple as laying down pride, bitterness, anger, hurt, whining, self-pity, and retaliation. When you have been hurt, your natural response is to fire back. But if you will holster your gun and walk in love, forgiving those who hurt you and trusting God for the outcome, you will have laid down your life for others just like Jesus did. Laying down your impulse to get even or punish someone for what they did is love in action.

Love is your nature, which means that loving is your behavior. Love is demonstrated in the way you treat other people. It is your attitude toward everyone you meet. Anyone you meet in this life should be able to identify you as a Christian just as easily as they determine whether you are a man or woman, girl or boy. A man looks, walks, and talks differently than a woman looks, walks, and talks. When you can't tell whether someone is a man or woman, you know something is not right with them. The same holds true for believers. Christians are children of a loving Heavenly Father and ought to be loving toward those around them. If they are not, you know there is something wrong with them.

How would someone know that you are a Christian? Would your behavior reveal that you are a Christian? John 13:35 tells us that people will know you are a Christian by your love. Great faith and great love working together will always reveal that you are a child of God.

A Man After God's Own Heart

He raised up unto them David to be their king; to whom also he gave testimony, and said, I have found David the son of Jesse, a man after mine own heart, which shall fulfil all my will.

Acts 13:22

God called David a man after His own heart. What does that mean?

David behaved himself wisely in all his ways; and the LORD was with him.
Wherefore when Saul saw that he behaved himself very wisely, he was afraid of him.
Then the princes of the Philistines went forth: and it came to pass, after they went forth, that David behaved himself more wisely than all the servants of Saul; so that his name was much set by.

1 Samuel 18:14-15,30

You cannot see into a person's heart, but you can observe attitudes and actions. David's behavior was marked by the fact that he behaved himself wisely. From this we can conclude that a person after God's own heart is someone who behaves wisely. The truth is, believers can talk about being the righteousness of God in Christ Jesus all day and all night. We can declare who we are in Him and talk about our authority over the enemy; but if we truly have a heart after God we will show good judgment and behave wisely.

Wisdom translates into good decisions and good behavior. Other people can judge us only by our behavior, by the fruit of our lives. Our true nature is on the inside of us, in our spirits; but our fruit is manifested on the outside, by how we behave. Fruit can be seen, touched, smelled, tasted, and heard by the physical senses. It can be assessed and evaluated by the natural mind. Since the world operates according to their physical senses and natural minds, that is what they will use to judge if we are Christians or not.

You don't need to be a botanist to know what kind of tree you are looking at if you can see the fruit it produces. If you see apples, you know it's an apple tree. If you see lemons, you know it's a lemon tree. If you see a person who shines with joy, encourages you when you are discouraged, prays for you in times of trouble, and pays your rent when you lose your job, you are probably observing a Christian.

David behaved himself wisely and had a reputation of exhibiting wise behavior. We know he walked in faith because without faith he would not have pleased God. We know he walked in love because faith works by love. Faith and love are behaviors that please God.

It All Begins at Home

I will behave myself wisely in a perfect way. O when wilt thou come unto me? I will walk within my house with a perfect heart.

Psalm 101:2

David declared that he would behave himself wisely within his house by having a perfect heart. Home is where it all begins. Home is where God wants you to start behaving yourself wisely, walking in love toward those who are closest to you. This is where you get the best practice. For example, if you sow love and goodness into your children, your faith will rise up to believe they will continue to live for the Lord even after they leave home. Love plants the seed; faith harvests the fruit.

The world does the opposite. They will show love and try to impress everyone except their family. They will work long hours and deny their spouse and children the love and attention they need. When they are at home they will take out all their frustrations and fears on those who are supposed to be the most dear to them. That is not the way anyone who has a heart after God will behave.

Like any behavior, walking in faith by love is learned. Once we are born again, we have the nature to love and the faith of God inside us, but it takes getting our minds renewed with God's Word to bring them out as fruit for others to see and partake of.

I had been out in the world for a long time, living a life of sin and selfishness. I wasn't raised with the love of God in my heart or any understanding of faith. When I got saved I had to cultivate these things.

For a long time it was very hard for me to believe God and walk in love when I got under financial pressure in caring for my family. I would think, *Lord, You're just going to have to do something because I don't know how we're going to make it. I don't know how I'm going to provide all the things we need. I want to do right by them, but it seems like every time I get ahead, something comes up with one of them and I'm back to zero again.*

That was when the Lord gave me the revelation about love being a behavior rather than a feeling. He showed me in the Word that my wife and my children are His gifts to me, and when I began to be grateful to Him for them, love conquered my fears and my faith was free to believe I would receive what I needed to provide for them.

> *Whoso findeth a wife findeth a good thing, and obtaineth favour of the LORD.*
>
> Proverbs 18:22

> *Lo, children are an heritage of the LORD: and the fruit of the womb is his reward.*
>
> Psalm 127:3

When I started looking at my wife and children as gifts from God who brought favor and reward to me, I started enjoying them more as blessings instead of seeing them as burdens that might hold me back or pull me down. I also began to see them as fertile ground where I could sow seeds of love. Then my faith would not be hindered when it came to believing God for everything I needed to provide for them and to protect them.

Faith, Sowing, and Reaping

Among the many facets of the life of faith is living by God's law of sowing and reaping. As the head of my family, I needed to understand this law in order to please God.

While the earth remaineth, seedtime and harvest, and cold and heat, and summer and winter, and day and night shall not cease.

Genesis 8:22

Planting and harvesting. Seasons. Temperature changes. Day and night. All these things will continue to function as long as the earth exists. And faith is an integral part of God's law of sowing and reaping. His love sows faith into our new, born-again spirits. We receive His love and all His blessings by faith. Then we go out and imitate Him by sowing in love and reaping by faith. This is the economic system of the Kingdom of God. Sowing and reaping. Giving and receiving. Love and faith.

Love gives. Faith receives. Love plants. Faith harvests.

Some people have made the mistake of trying to receive by faith without understanding the principles of love and giving. In the Kingdom of God it takes both love and giving in order to receive. It takes both because before there can be a harvest, there has to be a planting. Before there can be receiving, there has to be giving. And so before faith is going to be able to receive something, love has to sow something for God to multiply.

Second Corinthians 9:7 says that God loves a cheerful giver, because if you're not cheerful, you're not giving in love. After all, how can you have any faith in Him to bring a harvest when you plant your seed from a hard heart of compulsion or resentment? God doesn't want you to give as a compulsion, under coercion, or because you feel obligated. Then you become a religious robot or a victim of extortion. He wants you to give joyfully and willingly. That is the perfect heart David was talking about, a wise heart that is filled with love and faith.

I began seeing my family as a gift from God that brought me great pleasure and prosperity. I stopped feeling obligated to take care of them simply because I was the head of the family and instead began to look forward to any opportunity to plant seeds of love into their lives. Being the head of the family became a joy and a privilege instead of a heavy weight.

I like to prove the things the Lord reveals to me, so I decided to sow some seed for a need that I had. I had about five hundred dollars saved up in my wallet, so I went to my wife and said, "Honey, I want you to agree with me."

She said, "Okay. About what?"

I said, "I want to sow some seed, and I believe you are the best ground I know. Here's five hundred dollars, and I just ask you to agree with me for the harvest."

She said, "All right! I'll agree with you."

For weeks around my house it was as though I hung the moon!

Soon people began walking up to hand me money or mailing me a check to bless me. I had two thousand dollars in just a few days, which was what I needed. Praise God! I behaved myself wisely by giving cheerfully. My faith was rooted and grounded in love, and the seed I planted had to bring a great harvest.

This revelation of love and giving came to me while reading a very familiar Scripture.

God so loved the world that He gave his only begotten Son.

John 3:16

It is so easy to see love in action. God loved, so He gave. In a previous chapter I told you how I sowed into my kids by paying half the price of a car and they would pay the other half. Later on, when it was time for my son to get a better car, we went out to look. The amount of money I thought would buy a nice car was a whole lot less than what the dealers' wanted me to pay. In fact, it was more money than I had paid for my own car. I found myself thinking, *Lord, here I am ahead again. Now, I've got to do this, and it's going to put me behind.*

Once again the Lord reminded me that my family was good ground. He said, "Don't look at this as an obligation or something you've got to do. Instead look at it as an opportunity to plant your seed in good ground."

We sold my son's old car, and with the money from that sale and the money I had saved, we bought a great new car for him to drive. I told the Lord, "I'm going to invest in my son's life and do it cheerfully. I'm not going to look at this as a father buying his son a car out of obligation. I'm enjoying this as an opportunity to give something valuable to my son. I choose to behave myself wisely in this situation."

My son ended up with a great new car, and I was happy for him and so glad to have had a part in helping him. I sowed cheerfully and it was a great blessing to me. Then, the day after we closed the deal on that car, another blessing came to me. I got a letter from the mortgage company. I had refinanced my house months before to get a lower interest rate, and it seems the mortgage company owed me over two thousand dollars in insurance premiums I didn't know I had paid! I got a reward for having the right attitude and helping someone I love get the fulfillment of their dream.

The next time you have the opportunity to sow into the lives of your family, be wise and get excited about it! Let your love for them be the motivating factor for everything you do for them, and you will be surprised how your faith will rise up to reap great and marvelous blessings from God.

Don't Look at Anything Wicked

I will set no wicked thing before mine eyes: I hate the work of them that turn aside; it shall not cleave to me.

Psalm 101:3

David decided to act wisely by declaring that he wouldn't look at anything wicked. It is not wise to set any wicked thing before your eyes! You have to be careful about some of the stuff you watch on television, read in books, or see in movies because it will get on the inside of you and hinder your faith. You don't want anything to pull you out of the realm of love into the realm of worldliness, lust, fear, jealousy, and anger.

Keep thy heart with all diligence; for out of it are the issues of life.

Proverbs 4:23

The peace of God, which passeth all understanding, shall keep your hearts and minds through Christ Jesus.

Philippians 4:7

We have already seen how important it is to keep a heart of love in order for our faith not to fail, and the Bible tells us that the peace of God is what keeps our hearts and minds steady. Obviously, we are not going to have much peace if we are focusing our attention on evil, wicked things. And when we are caught up in lust, jealousy, fear, or anger, the love of God is overshadowed and can no longer guard our hearts and minds. We have become selfish and self-centered, walking according to the flesh instead of the Spirit. Then our faith fails.

I was born again and came into the light of God's Word when inflation was in double digits and interest rates were so high, I *had* to believe God because no one would loan me any money. No matter who is elected to government positions or what party is in power in America, my citizenship is in Heaven and I walk by faith in God and His Word. If, however, I set my eyes on what the government and our economy are doing and that becomes bigger than who I am in Christ and what I have as a joint-heir with Him, my heart can turn to fear and my faith will fail.

If you want to have the faith that pleases God, keep your eyes off of evil and wicked things! I understand that in the world today you can drive down the road and see something on a billboard that will offend you and tempt you all at once. If that happens, you haven't sinned; but you need to cast down that evil imagination immediately and get your mind and heart back on God's Word. Like Brother Hagin used to say, and there is a lot of wisdom in this, "You can't stop the birds flying over your head, but you can keep them from building a nest in your hair!"

The Faithful of the Land

Mine eyes shall be upon the faithful of the land, that they may dwell with me: he that walketh in a perfect way, he shall serve me.

Psalm 101:6

David knew that when you are developing the spirit of faith, walking in wisdom, striving to have a perfect heart at home, and setting no wicked thing before your eyes, those you choose as your companions will make a big difference in whether or not you are successful. *The Living Bible* translates verse 6, "I will make the godly of the land my heroes and invite them to my home. Only those who are truly good shall be my servants."

Ultimately, those you want to associate with are those you know by the Spirit. The Holy Spirit will bear witness in your spirit those who have caught the spirit of faith, and He will reveal to you those who are still walking primarily according to their senses, natural thinking, and emotions. The Apostle John admonished us in 1 John 4:1, "Beloved, believe not every spirit, but try the spirits whether they are of God: because many false prophets are gone out into the world."

In 2 Corinthians 5:16 the Apostle Paul said, "Wherefore henceforth know we no man after the flesh." Now that we are children of God, we know other people according to the Spirit and not according to the flesh. We put our emphasis on spiritual things rather than natural things when it comes to finding the "faithful of the land."

Peter walked with Jesus and knew Him personally for three and a half years. He was one of Jesus' closest companions, and he knew Him in the flesh. He slept near Him. He ate with Him. He watched Him. He was a member of Jesus' crusade team. He listened to all His sermons. Paul, on the other hand, never met Jesus or walked with Him in the flesh. Yet Jesus taught Paul, and Paul grew to know Jesus intimately by the Spirit. Peter said this about Paul:

> *Account that the longsuffering of our Lord is salvation; even as our beloved brother Paul also according to the wisdom given unto him hath written unto you;*
>
> *As also in all his epistles, speaking in them of these things; in which are some things hard to be understood, which they that are unlearned and unstable wrest, as they do also the other scriptures, unto their own destruction.*
>
> *Ye therefore, beloved, seeing ye know these things before, beware lest ye also, being led away with the error of the wicked, fall from your own stedfastness.*
>
> 2 Peter 3:15-17

One of the last things Peter wrote before he died was how important it was to study the writings of Paul. He said, "Some things are hard to understand, but every believer should study what he has written." Think about this a minute. Peter was saying this about someone who had not walked with Jesus in the flesh like he had, and he called him "our beloved brother Paul." Peter knew Paul by the Spirit.

Peter recognized that Paul had caught that same spirit of faith that he had caught from Jesus. They both caught it from Jesus, and then they imparted it to others whom they led and taught. That spirit of faith has been passed from generation to generation of believers through the centuries. Sometimes it seemed to almost disappear, but it certainly appeared again in our century in great men and women of God.

Again, the spirit of faith is caught not taught, and you catch it from being around people of faith who are the faithful of the land. First Corinthians 15:33 says that evil companions corrupt good manners. The *New American Standard Bible* says, "Do not be deceived: Bad company corrupts good morals." Who you spend your time with makes a tremendous impact on your life.

Just as your family is a gift from God, so are those who teach you and pastor you. When the Holy Spirit tells you, "This is your pastor, and this is the body of believers I want you to be a part of," you don't get up and leave because your friends or family say they don't approve, the pastor preaches something you don't like, or someone offends you. If anyone or anything tries to separate you from the gifts God has given you for your spiritual growth and well-being, they are not from God. You need to guard your heart and seek God if you have any question about where He has called you to attend church and fellowship with other believers.

Purpose to spend as much time as possible with those who have the spirit of faith. If you get offended or you offend someone (and this happens to every believer), forgive them, go to them, and try to reconcile with the person you are at odds with. If your pastor says something you don't understand or agree with, make an appointment to sit down and talk about it. My years of experience have taught me that no one knows everything and iron sharpens iron. Some of the greatest revelation and wisdom can come from getting into the Word with someone and allowing the Holy Spirit to settle a difference of opinion between you.

Be careful with whom you associate. Be particular about who you listen to and receive from. Be certain that you follow those who are faithful, who demonstrate their faith in word and deed. This will help you keep a perfect heart of love, walk in wisdom, and have faith that pleases God.

CHAPTER 16

Faith and Your Destiny

You are bigger on the inside than you are on the outside. This can work for you or against you, depending on what you choose to focus on. If your vision on the inside is not filled with the eternal things of God—His plans and purposes, His character and power—it can keep you from fulfilling your divine destiny and achieving any kind of happiness in life. There are many seemingly free people who are bound on the inside by their shortsightedness and lack of vision, usually as a result of how they were trained as they grew up.

A number of years ago I was given a dog. I had always wanted a Doberman pinscher, and one day my secretary gave me a little Doberman pup, six weeks old, which we named Samson (we called him Sam). Another staff member was very good at training dogs, and he loaned me a book about it. I had grown up with dogs, but training a Doberman was a little bit different, and I needed to learn some things.

One of the things I learned was that dogs are basically clean animals, especially when it comes to the area where they sleep. They will not mess it up. Therefore, I put Sam in a box by my bed and was careful to let him out regularly so he wouldn't have an accident. When he got bigger we got a bigger box, but eventually we couldn't find a box big enough. At that point I put up a barrier beside my bed, which gave him a little pen to sleep in beside me.

I taught Sam to lie down and to go to sleep while I was asleep, and he was very good about that. But then his legs got too long for the homemade pen, so I got a red leash and wrapped it around the bedpost at the foot of the bed, hooking it to his collar. It gave him enough room to get up, turn around, and change positions so that he was comfortable, but he couldn't go too far from the bed.

I'd say, "Sam, time to go to bed," and he would get up from the den or the living room and go to the bedroom, where he'd wait for me to hook his collar to the leash. I knew he could go all night without any problems, and he had proven himself to be a good dog, so after a few months I decided to let him go free at night.

I said, "Okay, Sam, it's time to go to bed," and he went into the bedroom and lay down next to the bed. I left the red leash on the bedpost just in case I ever needed to hook him up to it, but he was free. Sometimes he would wake me up at night when he got up and turned around, stretched, and got comfortable again. But he never moved from the area where the leash had confined him in the past.

I remember thinking, *Sam, you're a free dog and you just don't know it. You could sleep anywhere in the house, and I wouldn't know it. You could lie on the couch or sleep in any other room.* But because of his training, he wouldn't go past the length of that red leash.

The devil trains people the same way. Many people have a red leash of some kind. What is it that you were hooked to growing up that you still believe can hold you back? What is it that binds you and weighs you down? The goodness of God has overcome whatever that thing is. Jesus has set you free! And the Bible says that when Jesus sets you free, you are truly, forever free (John 8:36).

What Do You See?

There are many Christians who are bound to destructive habits and addictions, to fear and anxiety, and to all kinds of sins and problems they experienced in their past. The fact of the matter is, if they are born again, they are really not bound by anything except the love of Jesus Christ and their faith in Him. However, as long as they believe they can't do something, they won't be able to do it. As long as they see themselves as failures, they will continue to fail.

Vision on the inside is more important than what is seen on the outside. The Bible says that what is seen on the outside is temporary (2 Corinthians 4:18). Circumstances and situations are always subject to change, and they can be changed by the power of God. As a believer, it's what you see on the inside that is going to bring God's transforming power to bear in the situations and circumstances of life around you.

I read a story about a bear that was part of a traveling circus. This bear was kept in a cage that was twelve feet long by six feet wide, and he would walk twelve feet one way and then turn around and walk twelve feet the other way. All day long people would come to see him walk back and forth. Some people mocked him, poked him with sticks, and even threw cigarette butts into the cage just to watch him burn the pads of his feet when he stepped on them!

The bear adapted to his environment, never growling or trying to bite anybody. All he did was walk back and forth in his cage. That was his world until one day someone saw him and had compassion on him. It was arranged for this bear to be transferred to a zoo, where he would have a lot of space to roam, complete with green grass, water, and waterfalls. However, when his cage was set in the new area and the door was opened for him, all the bear did was to continue to walk back and forth in the twelve-foot path of his cage. When they finally prodded him out of the cage, he still continued to walk back and forth in a twelve-foot path.

Many times Christians are so conditioned to a life of lack, turmoil, and despair that they don't see anything else. Even though their redemption through Jesus Christ has opened the door to a whole new world of God's love and provision, they continue to walk in the same path. The Gospel is good news to anyone who has been abused and conditioned to a life of defeat. No matter how bound they have been the Word of God makes them free on the inside (John 8:32). They just need to bring that freedom from the inside to the outside.

> *The Spirit of the Lord is upon me, because he hath anointed me to preach the gospel to the poor; he hath sent me to heal the broken-hearted, to preach deliverance to the captives, and recovering of sight to the blind, to set at liberty them that are bruised.*
>
> Luke 4:18

Jesus is like that compassionate person who set the bear free so he could live out his life in peace with all his needs met. He redeemed us to free us from our cages so that we could live the *abundant life*. And yet so many believers are still walking in their little twelve-by-six-foot spaces, never venturing out in faith, never going through any open doors God gives them. How is it that so many people get saved and then stay content in their old cages? It's because they have more faith and feel safer and more comfortable in their cages than they have faith in the Creator of the Universe to keep them safe, healthy, happy, and prosperous. Too many times Christians settle for so much less than God has for them simply because they are afraid or unwilling to change!

The Dynamics of Change

Change can be frightening. Before you got saved, you probably didn't want to get saved. You might have thought those fanatical, born-again Christians were freaks, and the last thing in the world you ever wanted to be was one of them! But then one day you called upon the Name of Jesus and God imparted that measure of faith into you. With that brand-new faith, you received Jesus as your Lord and Savior and entered the Kingdom of God. Like that old bear, the door of your cage flew open and you found yourself walking out of darkness into light, a brand-new creature with a brand-new life.

If you are born again and you are still pacing in an old, familiar path of bondage, it is time to make more changes! You know you can do it because you have already gone through the biggest change a human being can experience. You have passed from eternal death and damnation to eternal life and peace. You have walked out of Satan's kingdom of darkness into God's kingdom of light. You have done this by faith, trusting in God's love, and that is exactly how you will make every other change for the better, now and in the future.

I saw a great example of this in 1986, when Kenneth E. Hagin conducted an All Faiths Crusade in Birmingham. People came from everywhere to attend, including me. There was a man who attended those meetings who, twelve years previously, had been a lawbreaker and had been involved in a shoot-out with the police. He had been shot, and a bullet had damaged his spine. The doctors had told him he would never walk again, and for twelve years he had been confined to a wheelchair.

Brother Hagin told everyone that Friday night was "Healing Night," and he would be laying hands on the sick then. He instructed everyone to attend the services and hear the Word in order to build their faith. He also advised everyone who could to wait until Friday night before getting into the healing line. The man in the wheelchair latched on to God's Word and the Word began to paint a picture inside him. He began to see himself walking. His inward man began to be renewed, and inside he got a vision of God's healing power being so much greater than any bullet, any doctor's opinion, any spinal damage, or any ache or pain.

The meetings started on Monday night, and on Tuesday night I met this man. You remember that 2 Corinthians 4:13 says, "We having the same spirit of faith, according as it is written, I believed, and therefore have I spoken; we also believe, and therefore speak." I perceived this man had caught the spirit of faith because he believed and he spoke, "Friday night is my night." Every time I went over to encourage him, he would say, "Friday night is my night! I'll be healed when hands are laid on me."

On Wednesday night during the service the Holy Spirit fell and three people just stood up and got out of their wheelchairs. This man was not one of them, but he just kept speaking, "Friday night is my night." Friday morning he came in and he said, "This is Friday, and tonight's my night." All day long on Friday he said, "Tonight is my night." God had planted a seed of a vision of healing inside this man. He was watering that seed, the Word of God, by confessing what the Holy Spirit was showing him on the inside: Friday night was his night to be healed. He started seeing himself whole, walking, without a wheelchair, no longer bound by an injury from the past.

I want to point out that this man must have also had a revelation of the love and forgiveness of God or his faith would have failed. The guilt and shame of his past would have convinced him he wasn't worthy to be healed. Satan must have told him time and time again that he was a criminal and didn't deserve to be healed, and that he deserved to be in a wheelchair the rest of his life or worse. But by the love and compassion of God, this man had a revelation that he was a new creature in Christ Jesus and all things were new. His past had been washed white as snow by the blood of Jesus. Therefore, he was free on the inside to receive the love of God and all the blessings of God, including divine healing.

To get where God wanted him, the changes this man had to make were monumental. He had to see himself and God in an entirely different way than he had seen God or himself before he was saved. And although I never spoke to him about it, I suspect that he went through a lot of criticism and skepticism from his family and friends before he got to the place where he could sit in that wheelchair and believe God loved him, had forgiven him completely, and wanted him totally healed.

That Friday night I was on the side of the auditorium where people in wheelchairs were seated. As Brother Hagin began to lay hands on those in the wheelchairs, the first ones he laid hands on made a feeble attempt to get up but nothing happened. When he got to this man, he just barely brushed the man's forehead with the tip of his fingers and that man sprang out of his wheelchair like a catapult had launched him!

That man walked up onto the stage on legs that hadn't been used in twelve years, and one of the ushers went to help him. But the anointing was so strong that night that the usher was having a hard time walking a straight line himself. As a result he managed to trip the man, and they both went staggering across the platform! The man never fell down, glory to God, and years later I saw him in another service. He was still walking and healed by the power of God.

This is just one example when I have witnessed the power of God setting people free when they were willing to change the way they thought, what they believed, what they said, and how they acted. There is nothing impossible to those who believe, and that insures that their divine destiny will be fulfilled.

Who Is God Looking For?

The eyes of the LORD run to and fro throughout the whole earth,
to shew himself strong in the behalf of them whose heart is perfect
toward him.

2 Chronicles 16:9

David was a man after God's own heart because he had a perfect heart. Was David perfect in all his ways? No, he was not perfect when it came to making good choices in life, but the Bible still says that he was a man after God's own heart. When all was said and done, David loved God more than anything and was quick to repent when he saw he had missed it.

The eyes of the Lord are running throughout this whole earth looking for people like David, whose hearts are perfect toward God. Why? So He can show Himself strong in their behalf. God found a man like that in 1986 in Birmingham, Alabama. That man got out of his wheelchair after twelve years of not walking and being told he would never walk again. God not only miraculously regenerated his spine, He also regenerated the muscle tissue in his legs that had atrophied and withered away to almost nothing. God taught him how to balance and how to walk again after twelve years of being confined to a wheelchair! What a testimony to the love and power of God! And He wants to show that same grace, love, and power toward every one of His children. He's looking for those who have caught that spirit of faith, who will take Him at His Word and speak and act like they believe it.

There is nothing that gives the Father more pleasure than finding His children in the spirit of faith and walking in love, power, and a sound mind. Not only can He bless them, but He can use them to do great exploits for His Kingdom. He can plant visions and dreams in their hearts that won't be hindered by fear or the bondages of their past.

What Does God Want Us to Do?

A man's heart deviseth his way: but the LORD directeth his steps.

Proverbs 16:9

We are to count the cost of what God has called us to do, giving thought and prayer to it, and then following the leading of the Holy Spirit. We must stay in the spirit of faith, mindful that the Lord will always provide everything we need. Not only does He plant visions and dreams in our hearts, but also He provides the means to carry them out. God doesn't always tell us every step from the beginning, so it takes faith to do the things He puts in our hearts. It's a mistake to try to figure everything out then strive to achieve our goals by our own reasoning and strength. What God would have us do is maximize our time with Him, rest in Him, and allow Him to order our steps each day. We must trust His wisdom and timing and let Him lead us, knowing that He loves us and wants us to succeed.

Because all the issues of our life are determined by what is on the inside of us, the most important thing God wants us to do is renew our minds with His Word and pray in the Spirit. This keeps our inward man focused on Him and His faithfulness. Then we will easily overcome any fear or frustration that might arise by the bondages of the past or our present circumstances.

If, on the other hand, we are not renewing our minds, we can spend a lot of time going nowhere fast. The natural man will quickly take over, and we will think, *If I'm not busy, I'm wasting time. If I'm not in motion somewhere, if I'm not going at it ninety miles an hour and making things happen, then I feel guilty and unproductive.*

Whenever you start thinking like that, stop and listen to the Lord. Take some time to get with Him and find out if you are in the right place doing the right thing. Then make any adjustments He tells you to make and continue walking with Him. One day you will wake up and see what marvelous things the Lord has done!

I know most people can't spend eight hours a day just praying in tongues, studying the Word, and ministering to the Lord, and He doesn't expect you to! He knows you have a job because He called you to that job. (If He didn't call you to that job, you need to find out where He's called you to be and get there.) God knows you have to go to work and be faithful there. He knows you have a family to provide for. And He knows how many hours there are in a day because He ordained that too. In fact, there isn't anything you experience in your life that Jesus hasn't experienced.

> *We have not an high priest which cannot be touched with the feeling of our infirmities; but was in all points tempted like as we are, yet without sin.*
> *Let us therefore come boldly unto the throne of grace, that we may obtain mercy, and find grace to help in time of need.*
>
> Hebrews 4:15-16

Knowing Jesus understands us makes it easy to go to Him for help. God didn't design us to do what He called us to do by ourselves. Our need for Him is built into us. Our need for our brothers and sisters in Christ is also built into us. He made us the "body" of Christ because we function together as one, with Jesus as our head. When we accept that we need God and we need each other, and that it is okay to need them, then we have no problem going to Him to obtain mercy and grace. And if God sends us to a brother or sister for assistance, we can go in faith.

When you put too much emphasis on your personal performance, or the Holy Ghost brings to your attention that you are focusing on the wrong things, back up, regroup, and take the time to let Him refocus your heart and vision. He may send you to an elder or a teacher to help you get through what you are experiencing at that time.

The Lord told me to stick close to Kenneth E. Hagin, to observe him and receive from him, and so I did. What stood out more than anything else about Brother Hagin was how he just took it easy. He didn't get in a rush about anything. Watching him over the years taught me how God wants me to act. He wants me to receive vision, cultivate it, incubate it, speak it into existence, and then just follow Him in it. I cannot make anything happen by my own efforts. I can only speak God's Word and follow the leading of the Holy Spirit, so there's no reason to get all bent out of shape about the timing of it.

When I was just a small boy I told everyone that I was going to go all over the world to tell people about God. Today I am traveling to countries around the globe preaching the Gospel and teaching God's Word to people. I never tried to make this happen. All I did was speak what God had put in my heart and walk in the steps He prepared for me to walk in from before the foundation of the world.

> *We are his workmanship, created in Christ Jesus unto good works, which God hath before ordained that we should walk in them.*
>
> Ephesians 2:10

God ordained the works that I have walked in and am walking in today. As I spoke His will and obeyed the Holy Spirit, doors opened to me, and I just walked through them. I never went knocking on anybody's door asking for a place to preach. I'm not saying there's anything wrong with that. I'm just saying that it is more important to speak the vision and rest in the Lord, knowing He will see to it that it comes to pass. Our part is to pray and obey in faith, confident of His love for us.

If God told me to build a church, I'd say, "Thank You, Lord! I've got vision for a church growing inside me. I commit this into Your hands because You said You would build Your church and the gates of hell would not prevail against it. I'll cooperate with You, but I'm not going to get in a hurry about anything. I'm just going to rest in Your Word and walk it through with You each step of the way." Isn't that so much better than working yourself into a frenzy and going through all manner of mental gymnastics about how to do what God told you to do?

Don't fall for the mistaken belief that it is only after you have completed what God called you to do that He is pleased with you. The Bible says that it is *faith* that pleases Him. He is pleased with you from the moment you are saved by faith and for all eternity after that. He is pleased with you because you are in Christ and He is pleased with Him. Every time you believe Him and His Word, speak words of faith, and act in faith, He just continues to smile at you with pleasure. He loves it when He gives you vision on the inside and you believe it, speak it, and trust Him until it comes to pass regardless of what is going on in the natural realm.

Faith That Won't Let Go

The spirit of faith you have caught is tenacious! There is something in you that will never stop pursuing the vision God has ordained and set before you. You have that bulldog faith when it comes to believing that what God has promised He will bring to pass. The spirit of faith just won't let go!

Jacob was an Old Testament example of someone who had that bulldog faith that wouldn't let go until he got the promise of God.

> *Jacob was left alone; and there wrestled a man with him until the breaking of the day.*
>
> *And when he saw that he prevailed not against him, he touched the hollow of his thigh; and the hollow of Jacob's thigh was out of joint, as he wrestled with him.*
>
> *And he said, Let me go, for the day breaketh. And he said, I will not let thee go, except thou bless me.*
>
> *And he said unto him, What is thy name? And he said, Jacob.*
>
> *And he said, Thy name shall be called no more Jacob, but Israel: for as a prince hast thou power with God and with men, and hast prevailed.*
>
> Genesis 32:24-28

Verse 28 in *The Living Bible* says, "Because you have been strong with God, you shall prevail with men." When we are strong with God, everything else falls into place. But what does it mean to be strong with God? If we look at Jacob, he just held on to God and wouldn't turn loose until he got the word, the blessing, he was looking for. A blessing is simply a good word from God.

Thank God, today we don't have to grapple with an angel! We don't have to grab hold of some supernatural being and keep him in a hammerlock until he blesses us! The Bible says that everything that pertains to life and godliness is ours in Christ Jesus. All we need to do is believe His exceeding great and precious promises and speak them out (2 Peter 1:3-4).

When God's Word becomes His personal letter to us and we meditate on His promises as our own, they get deep on the inside of us. They are written on our hearts. That is the same as Jesus personally sitting down with us and talking with us. That's much better than what Jacob had to go through!

The woman who was healed of the issue of blood, as told in the fifth chapter of Mark, also had faith that wouldn't let go. When she heard about Jesus and His love and mercy, she believed in her heart that He would heal her. Then she spoke what she believed, saying, "If I may touch but his clothes, I shall be whole" (Mark 5:28). Acting in faith upon what she had believed and spoken, she fought her way through a dense crowd of people and touched the hem of Jesus' robe. Instantly she was healed, just as she had said.

> *When she had heard of Jesus, [she] came in the press behind, and touched his garment.*
> *For she said, If I may touch but his clothes, I shall be whole.*
> Mark 5:27-28

It is interesting that the word translated as "touched" in verse 27 literally means "to attach oneself to."[1] This woman didn't just lightly brush her fingers across the hem of Jesus' clothes. She grabbed hold of that hem and wouldn't let go until she felt the healing virtue of God flow into her body and make her whole.

> *Jesus, immediately knowing in himself that virtue had gone out of him, turned him about in the press, and said, Who touched my clothes?*
>
> *And his disciples said unto him, Thou seest the multitude thronging thee, and sayest thou, Who touched me?*
>
> *And he looked round about to see her that had done this thing.*
>
> *But the woman fearing and trembling, knowing what was done in her, came and fell down before him, and told him all the truth.*
>
> *And he said unto her, Daughter, thy faith hath made thee whole; go in peace, and be whole of thy plague.*
>
> Mark 5:30-34

This woman was strong with God, and it gave her the strength to be strong with men, to make her way through that crowd until she received what she knew was hers as a daughter of Abraham. To fulfill your divine destiny, you need to decide to take hold of the visions and dreams God has put in you and refuse to let go.

It's All on the Inside

You cannot touch Jesus' clothing today, and angels aren't coming down to wrestle with you either. So how do you take hold of God?

> *God, who commanded the light to shine out of darkness, hath shined in our hearts, to give the light of the knowledge of the glory of God in the face of Jesus Christ.*
> *But we have this treasure in earthen vessels, that the excellency of the power may be of God, and not of us.*
>
> 2 Corinthians 4:6-7

Today we don't reach out and touch Jesus—because He is inside us! The light of the glorious Gospel of Christ is shining in our hearts. Jesus, the Living Word, is the treasure who lives in our earthen vessels. Now, instead of grabbing for something physically, we hold fast to the profession of our faith in Him.

> *Let us hold fast the profession of our faith without wavering; (for he is faithful that promised.)*
>
> Hebrews 10:23

The profession of our faith means faith speaks. What does the spirit of faith speak? We speak what we believe. What do we believe? The substance of things hoped for and the evidence of things not seen (Hebrews 11:1). In faith we believe and speak what God has promised in His Word, and we see it with spiritual eyes. The Bible gives us an entirely new way of thinking and speaking, a new language of the Spirit.

As believers we must learn the language of the Spirit because until we were saved we spoke the language of the world. The world speaks in terms of self, material things, and human understanding. The language of the Spirit is centered in God, thinks in terms of His Word, looks beyond the things that it sees with natural eyes into the realm of the spirit, and operates in God's wisdom and understanding.

When God gives us a vision or a dream for our lives, He gives it to us on the inside. We see it in our spirits and then we speak what we know is His will for our lives. This is what Abraham did when he received the promise that God had given him.

> *(As it is written, I have made thee a father of many nations,) before him whom he believed, even God, who quickeneth the dead, and calleth those things which be not as though they were.* ·
>
> Romans 4:17

We call those things that be not as though they are because we are not only the sons and daughters of Abraham, we are the sons and daughters of God. We speak His language, the language of faith. We do not consider physical circumstances and human limitations but instead are fully persuaded that God will perform what He has promised in His Word. We see it with spiritual eyes and speak it out of our mouths in faith.

When Abram began to introduce himself as Abraham, he was speaking a foreign language to the people who knew him. He was childless, too old to have children, and he was calling himself the father of nations! To their natural minds he was speaking nonsense. They didn't see what he saw on the inside. God's Word had planted vision of his being a father of many nations. In the spirit, through the eyes of faith, Abraham saw eternal substance in his hope. He believed what God said was his, and then he declared it.

Believers need to understand how powerful their words are when spoken from the revelation of God's Word and His will. In the Old Covenant the Holy Ghost lived in a box made of wood and covered with gold, and it was called the Ark of the Covenant. But today, in the New Covenant, the Holy Ghost lives in believers! And every time you open your mouth and let God's Word out, the same power is released as when they took the Ark of the Covenant onto the battlefield. The power of God is turned loose, the devil's plans and maneuvers are stopped in their tracks, and the things God has ordained for your life come into manifestation.

When you speak because you know you own something God has provided, even though neither you nor anyone else can see it with your natural eyes, God hears you. Words of faith spoken in agreement with God's Word activate His supernatural power to bring whatever is yours from the spirit realm into the natural realm. This is how you walk out your divine destiny by faith in God and His Word.

Jesus told His disciples to pray that God's will be done in earth as it is in Heaven (Matthew 6:10). He wanted them and everyone who prays that way to know that God wants things on earth to be as glorious for His children while they live on this earth as they are in Heaven. We should use our authority and declare God's will until it becomes reality in our lives, here on earth, just as it is in Heaven. If we don't speak it, it's not going to happen.

We can see God's will fulfilled in earth only by speaking words of faith. That is how God designed man to operate and bring His will to pass in our lives and in the earth today.

In Mark, chapter 16, Jesus commissioned believers to go into all the world, preach the Gospel, heal the sick, cast out demons, and speak with new tongues. The will of God becomes reality in the world today when believers who are bold in faith speak God's Word and declare, "It is written...."

Good things happen in the lives of Christians and all the lives they touch by faith in God. It is impossible to please God without it, so what are you waiting for? Dive into God's Word, catch the spirit of faith, and begin today to live the abundant life Jesus died to give you.

Endnotes

CHAPTER 1

Faith Works by Love

[1] James Strong, *Exhaustive Concordance of the Bible,* "Greek Dictionary of the New Testament," (Nashville, TN: Thomas Nelson Publishers, 1984), #26.

CHAPTER 2

A Heart of Love

[1] John Fox, *Fox's Book of Martyrs.* (Grand Rapids, MI: Zondervan Publishers, 1974), p. 5.

CHAPTER 4

Knowing God

[1] http://www.etymonline.com/index.php?search=crisis&search mode=none

CHAPTER 6

Your Right to Be Whole

[1] James Strong, *Exhaustive Concordance of the Bible,* "Hebrew and Chaldee Dictionary," (Nashville, TN: Thomas Nelson Publishers, 1984), #7495.

2 James Strong, *Exhaustive Concordance of the Bible,* "Greek Dictionary of the New Testament," #2390.

CHAPTER 13

Catching the Spirit of Faith

1 James Strong, *Exhaustive Concordance of the Bible,* "Greek Dictionary of the New Testament," #1411.

2 *Webster's New World College Dictionary,* Third Edition, Victoria Neufeldt, Editor-in-Chief (New York: Macmillan, Inc., 1996), p. 424.

3 Edgar J. Goodspeed and J.M. Powis Smith, eds., *The Bible: An American Translation* (Chicago: University of Chicago Press, 1931. 2nd edition, 1935).

CHAPTER 16

Faith and Your Divine Destiny

1 James Strong, *Exhaustive Concordance of the Bible,* "Greek Dictionary of the New Testament," #680.

Prayer of Salvation

God loves you—no matter who you are, no matter what your past. God loves you so much that He gave His one and only begotten Son for you. The Bible tells us that "Whoever believes in him shall not perish but have eternal life" (John 3:16 NIV). Jesus laid down His life and rose again so that we could spend eternity with Him in Heaven and experience His absolute best on earth. If you would like to receive Jesus into your life, say the following prayer out loud and mean it from your heart:

Heavenly Father, I come to You admitting that I am a sinner. Right now, I choose to turn away from sin, and I ask You to cleanse me of all unrighteousness. I believe that Your Son, Jesus, died on the cross to take away my sins. I also believe that He rose again from the dead so that I might be forgiven of my sins and made righteous through faith in Him. I call upon the Name of Jesus Christ to be the Savior and Lord of my life. Jesus, I choose to follow You and ask that You fill me with the power of the Holy Spirit. I declare that right now I am a child of God. I am free from sin and full of the righteousness of God. I am saved in Jesus' Name. Amen.

If you prayed this prayer to receive Jesus Christ as your Savior for the first time, please contact us on the Web at **www.harrisonhouse.com** to receive a free book.

Or you may write to us at:

Harrison House
P.O. Box 35035
Tulsa, Oklahoma 74153

About the Author

Reverend Scott Webb pastors Word of Life Christian Center in Birmingham, Alabama, which he founded in 1982 after attending Rhema Bible Training Center. From the beginning, excellence in ministry characterized the development of all aspects of Word of Life, including dynamic nursery, children's, youth, and outreach ministries. Stressing the integrity of God's Word, the church has grown and flourished.

Demonstrating a strong anointing in the area of faith and redemption, Scott Webb is in demand as he teaches in seminars, Bible schools, and church services throughout the world. His teaching always emphasizes the importance of the local church in the life and success of the believer. His daily radio program carries his practical and edifying messages nationwide.

Reverend Webb and his wife Phyllis are the parents of two children and grandparents of four. The entire Webb family resides in Birmingham and works alongside Pastor Webb in ministry.

To contact Scott Webb
Please write or call:

Scott Webb Ministries
100 Derby Parkway
Birmingham, AL 35210
Phone:(205) 833-8500
Fax:(205) 836-5348

E-mail: office@wordoflife.org

Website: www.wordoflife.org

Fast. Easy.
Convenient.

For the latest Harrison House product information and author news, look no further than your computer. All the details on our powerful, life-changing products are just a click away. New releases, E-mail subscriptions, Podcasts, testimonies, monthly specials—find it all in one place. Visit harrisonhouse.com today!

harrisonhouse

The Harrison House Vision

Proclaiming the truth and the power

Of the Gospel of Jesus Christ

With excellence;

Challenging Christians to

Live victoriously,

Grow spiritually, and

Know God intimately.